2.50

VINCI

MAUREEN HUNTER

For Sue,
with love + admiration
Maureen
April 2002.

"where there is great love
there are always miracles."
— Willa Cather.

Vinci
first published 2002 by
Scirocco Drama
An imprint of J. Gordon Shillingford Publishing Inc.
© 2002 Maureen Hunter

Scirocco Drama Editor: Glenda MacFarlane
Cover design by Terry Gallagher/Doowah Design Inc.
Cover art is a detail from Raphael's "The School of Athens"
Author photo by Earl Kennedy
Printed and bound in Canada

We acknowledge the financial support of The Canada Council for the Arts
and the Manitoba Arts Council for our publishing program.

Production inquiries (except Britain and Europe) should be addressed to:
Patricia Ney, Christopher Banks and Associates
6 Adelaide Street, Suite 610
Toronto, Ontario, Canada M5C 1H6
416-214-1155
cbanks@pathcom.com
Production inquiries for Britain and Europe should be addressed to:
M. Steinberg Playwrights
409 Triumph House, 187-191 Regent Street
London, England W1R 7WF
020-7287-4383
SteinPlays@aol.com

Canadian Cataloguing in Publication Data

Hunter, Maureen, 1947-
    Vinci
A play.
ISBN 1-896239-86-2
    I. Title.
PS8565.U5814V55 2002   C812'.54   C2002-900249-4
PR9199.3.H828V55 2002

J. Gordon Shillingford Publishing
P.O. Box 86, 905 Corydon Avenue, Winnipeg, MB Canada R3M 3S3

To Gary, with love
to Dennis Garnhum, with gratitude
and to the memory of my father

Maureen Hunter

Maureen Hunter's plays have been produced in Canada, the U.S. and Britain, and by CBC and BBC Radio. Her work has been nominated for two Governor General's Awards and two Dora Mavor Moore Awards (Outstanding New Play). Her plays include *Atlantis* (Scirocco Drama, 1997), *Transit of Venus, Beautiful Lake Winnipeg, The Queen of Queen Street* and *Footprints on the Moon*. A native of Saskatchewan, Maureen now lives on the banks of the Red River in Winnipeg.

Acknowledgements

This play was nearly five years in the writing, and for all I know I might be writing it still if it weren't for Dennis Garnhum. He led me out of the wilderness, and for this I'll always be thankful. He critiqued each draft of the play and, beginning in January 2001, worked with me intensively to help find the action of the story and to shape and focus it. His generosity and enthusiasm, his wit and wisdom and practical advice, made the creative process a joy. His challenge to write "three impossible stage directions" and his emphasis on the element of surprise were gifts that, along with his friendship, I will cherish.

I also wish to acknowledge in a special way the contribution made by Doug Evans, my highly-unpaid research assistant. His knowledge of history and his ability to uncover obscure details—from how a 15th century priest would carry his belongings to the damage done in Tuscany by a hurricane in August 1456—were a great help to me. He also inspired me, early in the process, by penning these lines:

> Leonardo was born—some place or other;
> His pa never bothered to marry his mother.
> To light up the earliest stage of his youth
> The wax of your candle is mostly surmise
> And only the wick is the truth.

Adriana Lombardini, my consultant on matters Italian, also deserves special thanks, as does Steven Schipper, Artistic Director, Manitoba Theatre Centre, for his continuing and valued support.

Others I wish to acknowledge for their generous and thoughtful comments and encouragement are Martha Brooks, Joan Horsman, Gary Hunter, Stephanie Kostiuk, Laurie Lam, Ustun Reinart, Dr. Carl Ridd and Judith Sharp. I'm grateful to Dr. Sarah McKinnon for suggesting pertinent research sources and to Marti Maraden, Artistic Director, National Arts Centre English Theatre, for her faith in this play.

I am deeply indebted to Dennis Garnhum, John Jenkins, John Munro and Gregg Coffin for their contribution to the premiere production, and to the actors who originated the roles of Bartolomeo, Piero, Antonio, Caterina, Francesco and Albiera, and whose comments and questions in rehearsal—and patience with revisions—helped to clarify and brighten the final draft.

Vinci was commissioned in 1997 by Manitoba Theatre Centre, which subsequently arranged two readings of the play, in December 1999 and May 2000. Additional funding was provided by the Manitoba Arts Council and the Canada Council. The play was workshopped in Toronto by MTC and the National Arts Centre in November 2001. I'm grateful to the organizations involved, to Dennis Garnhum and Kathryn Davies, and to the actors who participated in the readings and the workshop: Graham Ashmore, Sharon Bajer, Robert Benson, Derek Boyes, Ari Cohen, Paul Dunn, Patricia Fagan, Darcy Fehr, Patrick Galligan, Richard Hurst, David Jansen, Ross McMillan, Christian Molgat, Allan Perry, Alex Poch-Goldin, Gordon Rand, Kim Rannie, Anne Ross, Stephen Russell and Danielle Wilson.

Finally, I wish to acknowledge Ralph Waldo Emerson's description of the soul, which helped me to understand the play: "when it breathes through [man's] intellect, it is genius; when it breathes through his will, it is virtue; when it flows through his affection, it is love."

Sources Cited

Three books were invaluable in writing this play, providing background, details and, in some cases, actual lines used in the play: *The Merchant of Prato: Daily Life in a Medieval Italian City* by Iris Origo; *Eunuchs for the Kingdom of Heaven: Women, Sexuality and the Catholic Church* by Uta Ranke-Heinemann and *Medieval Popular Religion, 1000—1500, A Reader*, edited by John Shinners. Other books consulted, and from which certain lines may have been drawn, include *Culture and Society in Renaissance Italy 1420—1540* by Peter Burke; *Women, Family and Ritual in Renaissance Italy* by Christiane Klapisch-Zuber; *A Tuscan in the Kitchen* by Pino Luongo; *Wit and Wisdom of the Renaissance* by Charles Speroni; and various works on the period by David Herlihy, including *Tuscans and their Families: A study of the Florentine Catasto of 1427; Women, Family and Society in Medieval Europe* and *The Family in Renaissance Italy*. Of the many biographies available on Leonardo da Vinci, my favorite is *Leonardo: The Artist and the Man* by Serge Bramly. My research was extensive, but where necessary to enhance the story I have taken dramatic license.

Maureen Hunter
January 2002
Winnipeg

Setting

The play opens and closes in the refectory of the monastery of Santa Maria delle Grazie in Milan, on a November day in 1498. The balance of the play takes place in various locations in and around the village of Vinci in Tuscany, between April 1451 and August 1456.

For the premiere production, director Dennis Garnhum and designers John Jenkins and John Munro conceived and created a set which reflected the mind of Leonardo, and might have been designed by him. It was whimsical, magical, highly inventive and perfectly suited to the spirit of the play.

Characters

BARTOLOMEO, 30, a priest
PIERO, 30, a notary
ANTONIO, 60, Piero's father
CATERINA, 30, a servant
FRANCESCO, 20, Piero's brother
ALBIERA, 20, Piero's wife

(The ages given apply to the year 1456.)

Production Credits

Vinci premiered at the National Arts Centre, Ottawa, in co-production with the Manitoba Theatre Centre, Winnipeg, on January 10, 2002, with the following cast:

BARTOLOMEO .... Gordon Rand
PIERO .... Craig Erickson
ANTONIO .... Robert Benson
CATERINA .... Patricia Fagan
FRANCESCO .... Paul Dunn
ALBIERA .... Fiona Byrne

Directed by Dennis Garnhum
Set and Costume Design by John Jenkins
Lighting Design by John Munro
Original Music and Sound Design by Gregg Coffin
Assistant Director: Jean Morpurgo
Stage Manager: Kathryn Davies
Assistant Stage Manager: Michael Walton
Apprentice Stage Manager: Sally Crate

Vinci was originally commissioned by the Manitoba Theatre Centre, with support from the Manitoba Arts Council.

Leonardo was born in 1452—on Saturday, April 15, at 10:30 p.m., to be precise. Antonio, his grandfather, noted the event at the bottom of the last page in the notarial book that had belonged to Leonardo's great-great-grandfather. The entry reads: "1452: there was born to me a grandson, the child of Ser Piero my son." As was usual in the case of an illegitimate child, the mother's name was not recorded.

The few lines penned by Antonio tell us nothing at all about the house in which the child was born, the circumstances of his birth, or the way the birth was received. Nor do we know who took custody of the child—the paternal family or his mother. And who was this woman, whose surname is unknown?

— Serge Bramly, *Leonardo: The Artist and the Man*

Act One

Scene I

The refectory of the monastery of Santa Maria delle Grazie in Milan. Late on a November afternoon, 1498. On the upstage wall we see Leonardo da Vinci's "The Last Supper." The paint is so fresh it glows. BARTOLOMEO, as an old man, stands before the painting, utterly absorbed. In time he becomes aware of another presence in the room. He turns to the audience and addresses it as though it were this person.

BARTOLOMEO: *Perdonatemi,* I didn't hear you come in. You've come to see the painting. Of course, go right ahead. Take all the time you like. The monks won't mind at all and I'll— *(Flashes an irresistible smile.)* —be glad of the company. I'm the world's leading authority on this painting. *(With a charming gesture.)* No, of course I'm not. But I come here whenever I can. I come here so often the Prior feels I might as well just move in. Only yesterday he asked me if I'd like a cot brought down. To make it official, he said. He can't resist a dig. If he'd known the painting came with a priest attached, he'd have chosen an outside wall. A wall beside the garden. Then he could hand me a hoe! *(Laughs heartily; clears his throat.)* Monk humor. It may not seem funny to you, but at my age I can tell you there are few things sweeter than a little cheerful mischief between friends. But you came to see the painting. You mustn't let me intrude. Of art I know nothing at all. Only what I overhear. They're calling it a miracle. This painting—a miracle! Which I happen to know it is. But it gladdens my heart to hear it. I know the artist, you see.

He turns back to the painting. As he speaks, "The Last Supper" begins to fade away.

I come here, and I stand before this painting. But it's not the painting I see. Instead I see a woman— with a face as bright as sunshine—so many years ago. What was I? Barely twenty-five—and fresh from the bishop's school. My robe was so stiff and coarse, I remember, it chafed at the neck.

BARTOLOMEO becomes young as he speaks. He takes a book from a long-necked woven sack, containing everything he owns.

I didn't look much like a priest. I looked like I ought to be shoeing horses or tanning leather or pushing a plow. In truth, I looked like a peasant— which is what I was.

PIERO enters.

Piero was no peasant. We grew up together in Vinci. We had some wild times together, I can tell you. *(Opens the book.)* Stayed just this side of the law.

Scene II

A room in the da Vinci house in Vinci, April 1451. The kind of day when trees burst into leaf.

BARTOLOMEO: Listen to this, Piero, this is what I mean. *(Reads.)* Have you coupled with your wife from behind like a dog? If so, then ten days penance on bread and water. Have you coupled with her during her monthly cycle? Ten days penance on bread and water. Have you coupled with her after a child stirred in her womb or during the forty days before delivery? Twenty days penance on bread and water. Have you coupled with her on the Lord's Day? Four day's penance. Have you stained yourself with your wife during Lent? Forty days penance on bread and water—but if it happened while you were drunk, twenty days will suffice. Have you kept yourself chaste twenty days before Christmas? Every Sunday? During all fasts that the law ordains? On all feast days of the Apostles? On all major feast days? If not, forty day's penance on bread and water.

PIERO: Half the men in Tuscany would starve to death.

BARTOLOMEO: Can you imagine *me*—in the confessional—asking questions like that? And I have to do it.

PIERO: With a straight face.

BARTOLOMEO: I can't imagine it, even with strangers. And in Vinci? I hope they never send me here.

PIERO: Are they likely to?

BARTOLOMEO: You never know. Then there's a section on women. (*Hesitates.*) I shouldn't be reading you this, and you must swear you've never heard it.

PIERO: Sworn.

BARTOLOMEO: (*Reads.*) Woman is a misbegotten man. She has a faulty and defective nature. What she cannot otherwise get, she seeks to obtain through lying and diabolical deceptions. Woman is less qualified than man for moral behaviour—

PIERO: If only that were true.

BARTOLOMEO: For the woman contains more liquid than the man, and it is a property of liquid to take things up easily and retain them poorly. Hence women are inconstant and curious. When a woman has relations with a man—*(Stops reading.)*—he's warming to his topic now—*(Resumes.)*—she would like, as much as possible, to be lying with another man at the same time.

PIERO: This is beginning to get interesting.

BARTOLOMEO: Woman knows nothing of fidelity. If you give her your trust, you will be disappointed. *(Flips ahead; reads.)* And so, to put it briefly—*(Stops reading.)*—several pages later—*(Resumes.)*—one must be on one's guard with every woman, as if she were a poisonous snake or the horned devil. *(Closes the book.)*

PIERO: Do you really think you're cut out for the priesthood?

BARTOLOMEO: *(Miserably.)* That's what I'm trying to say. I ought to be able to believe in this—in *all* of this. And I've tried, but I honestly can't. It worries me.

PIERO: *(Moves next to him.)* Don't be offended, will you? I have to ask. How did this happen? The last time I saw you, you were going to be a mason—if you didn't run away to sea. I was astounded when my father told me you'd decided to become a priest.

BARTOLOMEO: *(Hesitates.)* You wouldn't believe me if I told you.

PIERO: Of course I would.

BARTOLOMEO: Let's just put it this way. Something happened which I—found I couldn't ignore. It's not a thing I talk about.

PIERO: But you can to me. Come, you know you can.

BARTOLOMEO: *(Glances at him; several beats.)* I had a vision of Saint Francis. He stood before me—in a blazing, golden light. He spread his arms, he said: You're needed. Then he disappeared. It happened very quickly. It was almost like a flash. I fell to my knees. I crossed myself. I was trembling like a newborn calf. I remember thinking: that was Saint Francis! And I don't know how I knew. And also I remember—as long as I live I'll remember!—the intensity of that light. How bright it was, how searing. The sense I had that if I touched it, my fingertips would be singed.

PIERO: *(After a moment.)* You can't be serious.

BARTOLOMEO: You see.

PIERO: It must have been a dream.

BARTOLOMEO: It was daylight, Piero. I was wide awake.

PIERO: You'd had a drop or two.

BARTOLOMEO: I wish I could say I had. I didn't believe in visions. Visions! They were for saints and hermits, not for people like me. I didn't know what to do. Didn't know whether to tell someone, or keep it to myself. Finally, I went to the priest. You remember Padre Gregorio? I went to him.

PIERO: And he talked you into it.

BARTOLOMEO: He simply said to pray. What do I pray for, Padre? He said: you pray for strength. He saw it as a calling. I saw it as a kind of death. I told him that. I wrestled with myself. It was an awful struggle. And then one morning I got out of bed—and I knew what I had to do. *(Turns to him.)* Your father spoke to the bishop for me. Did he tell you that? He put his neck on the line for me. I hope I don't let him down.

PIERO: You'll be all right, you know. All you need is a little practice—

BARTOLOMEO: Practice! I think I need more than that. I'm on my way to Barberino—a long week's walk from here. It's to be my first parish. My first parish! It makes

	my blood run cold. I'm afraid I'll be uncovered—as a kind of fraud. I'm afraid I'll be laughed out of town.
PIERO:	I felt the same when I was starting out.
BARTOLOMEO:	You don't have to say that.
PIERO:	I did. I only chose the law to please my father. Let me rephrase that. I didn't choose the law, my father chose it for me. Of course I felt like a fraud. Don't look at me like that. I could never bear to disappoint him. You know it as well as I.
BARTOLOMEO:	(Beat.) How is he, by the way?
PIERO:	Obsessed with finding me a wife.
BARTOLOMEO:	And has he found one?
PIERO:	God, I hope not. Yet. I've got a nice thing going in Pistoia with a judge's widow. I'm not ready to give that up. This woman is a wonder. The last time I was with her, we recited three psalms in the night, and two more in the morning. She nearly did me in. (No response.) Well? Aren't you going to chastise me? Assign me my penance? Padre?
BARTOLOMEO:	(In the same spirit.) Do you truly believe you've sinned?
PIERO:	Definitely not.
BARTOLOMEO:	There's not much point in it, then.
PIERO:	Seriously. This isn't going to come between us, is it?
BARTOLOMEO:	We've been friends a long time, Piero—
PIERO:	All our lives! You're like a brother to me. But suddenly I feel—oh, I don't know. I wonder if I know you, now you're wearing a gown.

BARTOLOMEO takes a playful swipe at him. PIERO parries. Another playful swipe, another parry. The horseplay has a ritualistic feel. It sets them laughing. But soon, as though they both know they've outgrown it, they fall silent.

BARTOLOMEO: Our lives are changing, Piero.

PIERO: They are.

BARTOLOMEO: I'm wearing a gown, and you'll be married soon. You *will* be married soon?

PIERO: I promised my father next year. If he can find the right prospect.

BARTOLOMEO: And what is that?

PIERO: That's the question, of course. On that we don't agree. He'd like a dowry the size of Monte Albano. I'd like breasts that size. We both know who's going to win. *(Stands; moves back to the window.)* I look at it this way: I have a year of freedom left. There's not a day of it I'm going to waste. *(Stares off.)* I've been thinking I may spend a lot of time in Vinci. In the next little while.

BARTOLOMEO: But your practice is in Pistoia.

PIERO: Nevertheless.

BARTOLOMEO: I don't understand.

PIERO: You haven't seen Caterina, then. My father's new maid. Well, she's not exactly new. I hadn't met her, though. She's a beauty, let me tell you. She has heft where heft should be. If you come here now and follow my gaze, you'll catch a glimpse of her. She's talking to Francesco at the far end of the garden. My God, what a sight.

BARTOLOMEO doesn't move. PIERO turns to him.

What's the matter with you? Don't tell me you're too pious now to even enjoy a look.

BARTOLOMEO: *(Quietly.)* Leave her alone, Piero.

PIERO: What did you say?

BARTOLOMEO: Leave her alone. You're going to be married soon. You have—*(With an edge.)* —the judge's widow. Keep your hands off that girl. You'll only ruin her.

PIERO: I'd like a chance to ruin her.

BARTOLOMEO: I'm serious.

PIERO: So am I.

BARTOLOMEO: *(Faces him.)* I want your word that you won't touch her.

PIERO: Not on your life!

> *BARTOLOMEO stands abruptly. He shoves his book angrily into his woven sack.*

There, you see what I mean? Already you've changed. You've become a dog in the manger—

BARTOLOMEO: That's not it at all.

PIERO: Fine. Then it's none of your business—if I have a go at her.

> *PIERO walks away. BARTOLOMEO charges him from behind. They fall to the ground. A serious fight ensues. BARTOLOMEO quickly has the upper hand. ANTONIO enters.*

ANTONIO: What's this now? *(Runs to them.)* Stop it! *(Tries to pull them apart.)* Stop it, for the love of God! What kind of priest is this?

> *This registers. As suddenly as he charged PIERO, BARTOLOMEO pulls away. He is deeply*

ashamed. He bends to help PIERO up, but PIERO shoves him away. He stands on his own. He is also very shaken. ANTONIO addresses them both.

What's the matter with you? One afternoon you have to spend together, and this is what you do!

BARTOLOMEO: *(Turns to ANTONIO.)* Antonio, I don't know what to say—

ANTONIO: Don't say it to *me*.

BARTOLOMEO: *(Turns to PIERO.)* Forgive me, Piero.

PIERO: *(With his eyes averted.)* Forgiven.

BARTOLOMEO: I'm ashamed of myself. I don't know what came over me—

PIERO: Ah, I pushed you too far. Never again, believe me. My God, what an arm you've got.

ANTONIO: What brought this on? I don't believe I've ever seen you fight. Not with each other, at least. *(No response; begins to move off.)* Well, make it up, the two of you. Then come to the garden. We're going to celebrate Bartolomeo's ordination. *(Turns back.)* You *were* ordained?

BARTOLOMEO: *(Bows his head.)* I deserve that, Antonio.

ANTONIO: I think perhaps you do. *(To PIERO.)* You won't keep us waiting?

PIERO: No, Father. We'll be right there.

ANTONIO exits. BARTOLOMEO faces PIERO.

BARTOLOMEO: Promise me you'll stay away from her.

PIERO: Bartolomeo—please!

BARTOLOMEO: If you could offer her a future, it would be different. You know you can't.

PIERO:	She might not even have me.
BARTOLOMEO:	Just in case.
PIERO:	*(Beat.)* You realize you have no right to ask this.
BARTOLOMEO:	I do, you know.
PIERO:	You don't. But all right, I give you my word. I do it out of friendship—
BARTOLOMEO:	Out of friendship, then.

> *They shake hands. PIERO places his left hand on top.*

PIERO:	For God's sake, Bartolomeo. If ever anything is going to come between us, let's not let it be a woman. That would be absurd. You with your vow of chastity and me—with my future sealed.

> *BARTOLOMEO places his left hand on top of PIERO's. It's a solemn moment. Then a gong is heard, off, breaking the spell. PIERO turns towards the sound.*

We're coming, Father! *(To BARTOLOMEO.)* That gong. One of these days, I swear to God, it's going to disappear. And all of Vinci will thank me.

> *They exit with their arms across each other's shoulders.*

Scene III

> *A room in the da Vinci house, a few weeks later. Nature at full throttle. PIERO enters, with a leather saddlebag. He sits at a desk or table, draws papers from his saddlebag, takes up a pen, begins to write. CATERINA enters, with a brush and pail.*

CATERINA:	Oh! I thought the room was empty. *(Turns to go.)*

PIERO: Don't go. I won't disturb you.

CATERINA: But I'll disturb you, I think.

PIERO: No, you won't, I swear it. I can work through anything. I mean it, Caterina. You'll offend me if you leave.

              She kneels reluctantly and begins to scrub the floor. He resumes his work. She keeps her head down; he does the same. Both are very tense.

PIERO: I didn't see you at the festival the other day.

CATERINA: No, I—didn't go.

PIERO: A shame. Everyone else was there. The village, and all the countryside. We danced until the stars had gone to bed.

CATERINA: Francesco said.

PIERO: We'd have danced you off your feet, Francesco and I, if you'd come. Do you like to dance, Caterina?

CATERINA: Of course.

PIERO: I thought you probably did. I watched for you all evening. Kept thinking you'd appear. I even picked some flowers for you. All the women—did Francesco tell you?—wove flowers through their hair. You'd have looked very nice like that. *(Without looking up.)* It wasn't because of me you stayed away. Was it, Caterina?

CATERINA: *(Uncomfortably.)* Why would it be?

PIERO: I couldn't think of any other reason why you'd miss a dance.

CATERINA: I might have been ill, you know.

PIERO: That's true, you might have been. But you looked so well in the morning. You looked—quite radiant.

She's at a loss for words. He suddenly throws down his pen.

I don't know what I'm doing here, I swear to God I don't. I ought to go back to Pistoia. Now, immediately! I shouldn't hang around here. But I do. Can't help myself. Keep making up excuses not to leave. I don't know what I'd do if I couldn't see you, that's the problem. I seem to need to see you every day. Even a glimpse will do. *(Laughs self-consciously.)* I never thought I'd hear myself saying such a thing. Never thought I'd get up in the morning with such heady expectations! Will I see her? When will I see her? What will I say, if I do? Will she look at me or keep her face averted? Will she ever smile? You smile at Francesco, I notice. But you never smile at me. *(Two beats.)* I think you're afraid, Caterina. You want to smile at me, but you won't let yourself. You won't even let yourself look.

He can't stand it any longer: he has to look at her.

I think if you actually looked at me—just looked at me—and smiled. I think I could go away. At least for a little while. And if you were to touch me... who knows how long I'd be gone? *(Emphatically.)* Do you want me to leave, Caterina? If you do, then look at me.

She's caught between a rock and a hard place; she doesn't know where to turn. He stands abruptly.

Caterina—

CATERINA: No, I don't want you to leave! And yes—I want you to. Don't come any closer! I'll run out of here if you come any closer.

PIERO: *(Freezes.)* I'm a pillar of stone.

CATERINA: Everything you've said is true. I am afraid. We could get in trouble, you and I—

PIERO:	We could. *(Pause.)* It wouldn't be the worst thing in the world—
CATERINA:	It would!
PIERO:	Of course it would.
CATERINA:	It isn't how I see my life unfolding.
PIERO:	No, I'm sure that's true.
CATERINA:	My father always told me: God has a plan for you. Seek it, Caterina! Find it! Don't rest until you know. Well, I haven't found it, but I feel quite certain— *(Breaks off.)* I've seen it so often, you know. Perfectly sensible girls who simply tossed away their futures. Nine months later—*(Indicates a huge belly.)* No. That's not for me. *(Turns away.)* I lie in bed at night and I can't sleep for thinking of you. I'd sell my soul for a kiss! But in the morning, in the cool clear light, I manage to recover my resolve. I can't let go of that. I can't! You understand that, I hope?
PIERO:	*(After a struggle.)* Yes, I understand. You're very wise, Caterina. Very—responsible. As for me, I have commitments. I do have—*(With an edge.)* —commitments. Which I've sworn to keep.

He takes his seat again. A pause.

CATERINA:	We're agreed, then, are we?
PIERO:	We are. *(Takes up a pen.)*
CATERINA:	There'll be no need to feel—uncomfortable, together—
PIERO:	No, that's behind us now. I'm glad we had this conversation, Caterina.
CATERINA:	So am I. I feel so much better!
PIERO:	Yes, me too.

They both resume work. Long pause. The tension grows again.

All things considered, though, it might be best for me to get away from Vinci.

CATERINA: Now, you mean?

PIERO: The sooner the better, I think. *(Stands.)*

CATERINA: Oh, but—*(Makes a sudden movement, knocks the bucket over, spills the water.)* Oh!

PIERO: *(Moves to her.)* Here, let me help you with that.

CATERINA: No! You mustn't—I can—

PIERO: *(Kneels in front of her.)* Please!

> *He holds out his hand for the brush. Their eyes collide. She kisses him passionately. This leads to a wild embrace. Soon they're rolling on the floor. FRANCESCO enters. He stops dead when he sees them. They pull apart. They stand.*

PIERO: Francesco—

> *CATERINA suddenly bends, picks up the bucket and flees.*

I wonder if you could persuade yourself to put that out of your mind. Father would be disappointed, and I wouldn't want to—

FRANCESCO: No.

PIERO: She's so beautiful, Francesco. Takes the breath right out of me.

FRANCESCO: *(Two beats.)* Your clothes are sopping wet. You'd better change. Father wants to talk to you. He's had an answer from the Amadori family. The ones with more daughters than they can count. More money too.

Piero:	*(Hesitates.)* I'm sure you think I'm—
Francesco:	No, I'm sure I don't.

PIERO still seems uncertain.

Piero, you're my brother. Go.

Satisfied, PIERO exits. FRANCESCO stands staring at the wet mark on the floor.

Scene IV

A room in the da Vinci house, five months later. Everything in Tuscany is ripe. FRANCESCO stares into space. CATERINA enters, with a basket.

Caterina:	I've been looking everywhere for you! Now I find you staring into space. What are you thinking about?
Francesco:	Nothing.
Caterina:	I know that isn't true. I know your head is full of things, clamoring to get out. Lately you've been locking them inside. It isn't good for you. It furrows your brow and turns your face all dark and gloomy—like the statue of Saint Francis in the church. *(No response.)* No smiles this morning, either. Aren't you feeling well?
Francesco:	*(Moves to a chair.)* I'm fine. I like to be left alone, sometimes. *(Flops down.)* Like anyone else.
Caterina:	*(Sets down the basket.)* I can't leave you alone, Francesco. Not today. I need your help.
Francesco:	I'm tired of lugging things around.
Caterina:	That isn't what I meant.
Francesco:	*(Turns away.)* I'm sick and tired of Vinci. I want to go away.

CATERINA: When the time is right, I'm sure you will.

FRANCESCO: I'm sure I won't.

CATERINA: You will. You'll go to university, like Piero did.

FRANCESCO: Why would I do that? I'm not the one—*(Mimics his father.)* —on whom the future hangs.

CATERINA: What's that supposed to mean?

FRANCESCO: Second sons don't go to university. Not in the da Vinci family. Not in two hundred years! Second sons stay home, and mind their manners, and wait to be married off. That's the way it is. You might as well be a girl as a second son, for the all the rights you have. Might as well be a bastard.

CATERINA: What's the matter with you? We used to be friends, remember? Now you keep running away. If I enter a room, you leave it. If I smile at you, you frown. I know I've hurt your feelings—

FRANCESCO: Well, you haven't. So that's that.

CATERINA: It's because of Piero, isn't it? Piero and me. You saw us together that day in the spring—

FRANCESCO: I didn't see anything.

CATERINA: You're sure about that, Francesco?

FRANCESCO: Definitely.

CATERINA: And all these months, you've noticed nothing.

FRANCESCO: Nothing to notice.

CATERINA: I see. *(Carefully.)* It's going to be hard to explain to you, then—how I've come to be carrying his child.

             FRANCESCO stands.

             I don't know if you'll believe me. Maybe no one will. I didn't expect this to happen. It shouldn't

	have. *(Grows upset.)* There are ways around it, you see, that women talk about—that I've overheard. So I knew what I was doing. I thought I knew!
FRANCESCO:	I believe you, Caterina.
CATERINA:	What a fool! *(Struggles to stay in control.)* I've got to get word to Piero. I don't know where else to turn. I have to talk to him, I have to tell him. I can't think of anything else! I heard your father saying he was putting a package together—to send to Piero, he said. Could you slip a letter in, Francesco? I don't dare try it myself.
FRANCESCO:	Of course I can.
CATERINA:	Without your father knowing.
FRANCESCO:	Father? God forbid.
CATERINA:	Just tell Piero that I have to see him. As soon as possible!
FRANCESCO:	I will, Caterina. I will.
	A pause. CATERINA takes a packet from her pocket.
CATERINA:	Here, take a whiff of this.
	He does. It nearly knocks him over.
	Good. It's not just me.
FRANCESCO:	Where on earth did you get that?
CATERINA:	I went to see Bianca. I haven't been feeling so well. I'm supposed to wear it close to my heart, but the smell is too much for me. *(Puts the packet away.)* So I keep it here. At night I slip it underneath my bed. And say a prayer to Saint Margaret. That's what she said to do.
FRANCESCO:	You shouldn't be going to Bianca. She's a witch.

CATERINA: She's not a witch.

FRANCESCO: Father says she is. She has a look that could darken a mirror. That's what he always says.

CATERINA: I will admit she knows things—long before they occur. She dreamt of my child, Francesco! She dreamt of him weeks ago. She knew I'd be coming to see her. Isn't that strange? I said if that's the case, she might have had the packet ready. She might have saved me the wait! She didn't seem to find that funny… *(Trails off.)* She did dream about him, though—the son she says I'll have. A very powerful dream.

FRANCESCO: What was it, Caterina?

CATERINA: I promised not to say. Besides, who knows with dreams? Sometimes we fool ourselves. When I first began to love Piero, I had the sweetest dream. I went to the door one morning, and on the step were flowers. In a little vase. I turned and there was my father—as alive as you are now. He wagged his finger at me as he often used to do. His finger said—Be Careful, but his eyes said—Good for you! *(Beat.)* I thought I had his blessing. Maybe I didn't, at all! *(Struggles again for control.)* I don't know what will happen to me now. Do you?

FRANCESCO: *(Considers this seriously.)* No.

CATERINA: *(Smiles in spite of herself.)* That's why I like you, Francesco. You call a thing by its name. My father was the same. I asked him once, when I was very small, to describe the day I was born. I was hoping for a pretty story. Do you know what he said? You were born the day the white ox died, that I bought from Meo the Lame. At dawn I found him feet-up in the shed—the ox, that is. At dusk the midwife came, and you slipped screaming out. Death opened the day, he said, life closed it. I rejoiced for both of you.

She smiles at him. He can't bring himself to smile in return.

Don't worry about me, Francesco. I'm tougher than I look. Tougher than anyone imagines. A heart like old leather, in here.

Still no response. She picks up the basket.

You'll be sure to write that letter?

FRANCESCO: I'll do it now.

CATERINA exits. FRANCESCO turns away. He finds himself face-to-face with ANTONIO.

Scene V

The da Vinci garden, moments later. CATERINA is raking leaves. ANTONIO strides on. FRANCESCO trails after him.

ANTONIO: You're absolutely certain, are you?

CATERINA: *(Glances at FRANCESCO.)* Certain?

FRANCESCO: I'm sorry, Caterina!

ANTONIO: Are you absolutely certain that the child is Piero's? Look me in the eye and tell me. Swear it!

CATERINA: *(Looks him in the eye.)* On my father's soul.

ANTONIO: *(Two beats.)* Then I'll tell you what happens now. As of this moment, it's over. You won't be together again. I'll go to Pistoia tomorrow. I'll give Piero the news. You may be thinking he'll refuse to give you up. He won't refuse. I know my son and I can tell you: he knows where his duty lies. He has a bright career ahead of him and if he marries well—

FRANCESCO: Father.

ANTONIO: As I intend to see he does—

FRANCESCO:	Father!
ANTONIO:	*(Turns on him.)* Don't you dare interrupt! There have been secrets kept in this family, and you've been part of that. I'm disappointed in you, and I'm deeply—*(Turns back to CATERINA.)* —disappointed in Piero. Yes, and also in you. I promised your father I'd look after you. What would I tell him now? What would you tell him yourself, if he were here to listen? My God, this would break his heart!
CATERINA:	He always told me I should seize whatever gave me joy—
ANTONIO:	I doubt if he had this in mind!

CATERINA turns away. ANTONIO tries to get himself in hand.

	You'll have to find a new position, that's all there is to that. I'll help you, of course. It may take a month or so to get you settled, but you needn't worry. I have friends I can turn to. I'll do right by the child, as well. You have my word on that. Once it's born, I'll make arrangements—
CATERINA:	*(Turns back.)* What are you talking about?
ANTONIO:	I'll see that you're not saddled with a child. Where are you going?
CATERINA:	I'm leaving.
ANTONIO:	I haven't dismissed you.
CATERINA:	I quit! *(Beat.)* I'll find my own position.
ANTONIO:	What kind of talk is that? You won't find anything, in your condition. Not without my help.
CATERINA:	I don't want your help.
ANTONIO:	You say that now. You'll change your mind.

CATERINA: I won't. *(Directly to him.)* I won't.

ANTONIO: Now listen, Caterina. You don't know the world. A woman with a child—an unmarried woman—isn't welcome everywhere. Some would say she isn't welcome anywhere. A month ago, in Firenze, they drowned a girl like you. A friend of mine saw it happen. They drowned the baby with her. A little boy, he said, no bigger than a cat. They bound the two of them together, the mother's arms around the baby, and threw them off the Ponte Vecchio.

CATERINA: *Madre di Dio! (Crosses herself.)*

ANTONIO: Let me find a new position for you. Where I know they'll look after you. And then, if you come to your senses—once the child is born—

CATERINA: I've come to my senses. *(Exits.)*

ANTONIO: That child is a da Vinci, no matter what you do! Caterina?

> *Two beats. He turns to find FRANCESCO staring at him.*

Don't look at me like that. I'm responsible for this family. I have to make decisions—for the common good. My father did it, and his father did it. Someday you'll do it too.

> *ANTONIO exits.*

Scene VI

> *A house up the mountain from Vinci, April 1452. A glimpse of towers and rooftops, poking through the mist below.*

BARTOLOMEO: *(As an old man.)* Caterina found a position in a house up the mountain from Vinci. It wasn't much of a house. Nothing like where she'd been. Did she hope Piero would come to her, and carry her away? Did she find herself watching for him? Did she gaze down at the roofs and towers of Vinci, poking through the mist, and wonder when he'd appear? If she did, she never said.

A soft rain begins to fall.

On the fifteenth of April—the following spring— the midwife Bianca climbed up Monte Albano through the early morning fog. The household was astonished—no one more than Caterina—but Bianca was right again. By evening the child was born. A boy. A strong and healthy baby boy.

CATERINA enters, with a child's toy.

When word of the birth reached Vinci, Antonio made note of it. In a kind of diary he kept. There was born to me a grandson, he wrote, the child of Piero my son. He didn't mention the mother's name at all. *(CATERINA exits.)* He was, perhaps, preoccupied. After all—

Church bells peal. Flowers burst into bloom. The church in Vinci appears. PIERO enters, in wedding attire. He stands waiting nervously. A door opens in the distance and a carpet of sunlight streams toward his feet. In the doorway stands ALBIERA, in a wedding gown. BARTOLOMEO moves to the church.

Everyone assumed Piero would now do his duty— stock the cupboard and the cradle—that his new wife Albiera would do hers. The house would fill with children…

ALBIERA glides up the carpet of sunlight. When she reaches PIERO, they exit. BARTOLOMEO closes the door.

On their wedding night, as was the custom, a doll

was laid in the conjugal bed. To promote fertility. Not that it would be needed. A little insurance, that's all. As for me, I was busy. Fumbling my way through the first years of my priesthood. Leaving an unlasting impression on my parishioners. *(Becomes young as he speaks.)* Then the thing I'd dreaded came to pass. I was told to return to Vinci—as the parish priest. *(Wipes his brow.)* It was August, I remember. Hot as flame. Nothing seemed the same. The church looked smaller, the Via Roma narrower. Even Monte Albano seemed to have shrunk a bit. As though it had huddled down amongst the hills around it, so as not to draw attention to itself. There were other things. The Vinci I remembered was a tranquil, timeless place. That had changed.

FRANCESCO enters.

I hadn't even reached the village when it started.

FRANCESCO: Welcome back to Vinci, Padre!

BARTOLOMEO: Francesco! All grown up.

FRANCESCO: I've been watching for you. I thought you'd never come! Father wants to see you. Right away, he said.

BARTOLOMEO: Why? What's happened?

FRANCESCO: You'll find out, soon enough. *(Leans in.)* You'll have to hear him out, of course, but just between you and me: I hope you won't be riding in his nether pocket, like the last priest was. *(Takes BARTOLOMEO's woven sack, containing everything he owns.)* I'll drop this at the church for you. You'd better go straight to him. He's waiting for you in his garden—and you know how he hates to wait.

They exit together.

Scene VII

> The da Vinci garden, immediately following. A cool oasis on a blinding August day. We hear cicadas and the trill of birds. On a table sits a hammer and a small brass gong. ANTONIO paces. BARTOLOMEO enters.

ANTONIO: There you are, Bartolomeo! *(Takes his hand.)* But I mustn't call you that. It has to be Padre now, doesn't it? Catch me if I slip up.

BARTOLOMEO: It's good to see you, Antonio. It's been a long time.

ANTONIO: It's been much too long. *(Still clinging to his hand.)* In fact, I'm annoyed with you. You haven't been to see us once in all this time. Five years! You've been negligent.

BARTOLOMEO: They've kept me very busy. And always on the move. I haven't spent a year in any parish—*(Breaks off.)* Antonio?

ANTONIO: When I look at you I suddenly see Piero, standing at your side. A couple of strapping boys! I'll tell you frankly, Padre, it brings a tear to my eye.

BARTOLOMEO: Don't tell me you've grown sentimental.

ANTONIO: Is there any way else to grow?

BARTOLOMEO: *(Smiles.)* How is Piero? And when can I see him?

ANTONIO: *(Drops his hand.)* Who knows? *(Moves away.)*

BARTOLOMEO: That's not much of an answer.

ANTONIO: He's expanded his practice to Firenze, to Pisa. He's hardly ever home. *(Glances at him.)* I exaggerate. He drops in for a day or two, every once in a while. We have to be content with that. *(Sits.)* Come and sit with me. I want to rest my legs. I'm building a wall at the far end of the garden. It's wearying work.

BARTOLOMEO: Your garden has flourished since I saw it last. *(Sits next to him.)*

ANTONIO: It ought to have. I've poured my life's blood into it, the last few years. I rarely even leave it now, except for mass on Sundays. *(Pointed.)* If the sermon's worth the walk.

BARTOLOMEO: I'll see what I can do.

ANTONIO: That's what I like to hear. *(Takes up the hammer.)* Now. There's something I want you to sample— *(Strikes the gong.)*—and you're not allowed to refuse. I could offer you wine, of course. But I've sent for something even better.

BARTOLOMEO: Which is—?

ANTONIO: Marjoram. My own special brew. It stimulates digestion, soothes the nerves, cures colds, eases headaches and relieves flatulence. I'll send some down to the church for you.

BARTOLOMEO: Thank you, but I—

ANTONIO: Don't decline it, please. It's always good to have on hand. Marjoram cures everything—

                ALBIERA enters, with two cups. They turn towards her.

                Except a broken heart. And I'm sure you don't have one of those. You haven't met our Albiera, have you? Piero's wife.

                BARTOLOMEO is taken aback; this is not the kind of wife he had imagined for PIERO. But he recovers quickly. He stands and takes her hand.

BARTOLOMEO: I'm very pleased to meet you.

ALBIERA: I'm so glad you've come. I hope you can help us, Padre. We're counting on that! The last priest meant well enough, I think, but—

ANTONIO:	*(Takes the cups.)* Yes, yes, child. Depart.
	ALBIERA exits. ANTONIO, looking very gloomy, stares after her.
	Female chatter is the scourge of the new age. Don't you agree?
BARTOLOMEO:	Actually, I haven't—
ANTONIO:	Been exposed to it, I guess.
BARTOLOMEO:	*(Sits next to him again.)* I was going to say I haven't found that to be true. Though certainly the Church decries it. More, perhaps, than it should.
ANTONIO:	She chatters out of nervousness. The more nervous she is, the more she chatters—and she's a very nervous girl! If I let her start she never stops, so I try not to let her start. It must seem rude, but I confess—I don't know what else to do. Drink it up now, while it's hot.
	BARTOLOMEO takes a reluctant sip. ANTONIO stares at his cup.
	My wife, you see, was always very quiet. Remarkably serene. She moved about the house as silently as a ghost. But then she was content, you see, whereas Albiera—*(Breaks off.)*
BARTOLOMEO:	Yes?
ANTONIO:	*(Drains his cup, sets it down.)* Bartolomeo—*Padre*—we have a problem here. We need your guidance—and your intervention.
BARTOLOMEO:	I'll do whatever I can.
	ANTONIO hesitates. He glances after ALBIERA.
	Is it Albiera? Is she the problem?
ANTONIO:	I'd hate to put it that way. Poor Albiera. She feels

she's disappointed everyone. And of course she has.

BARTOLOMEO: How, Antonio?

ANTONIO: *(With the weight of doom.)* Four years married and no children. The girl is barren. Her sister Alessandra, on the other hand, delivers one a year. If Piero had done as I suggested—*(Breaks off.)* But it's much too late for that.

BARTOLOMEO: It's a disappointment, surely. But I don't believe it necessarily follows that the girl is barren.

ANTONIO: Why not?

BARTOLOMEO: You just finished saying that Piero is seldom home.

ANTONIO: He's home—*(With a wave of his hand.)*—enough. Enough to do his duty. No, it isn't that.

BARTOLOMEO: Perhaps he's incapable of fathering a child.

ANTONIO gives him a look.

It's possible, you know.

ANTONIO: My son is not incapable. You have my word on that.

BARTOLOMEO: I don't mean to offend you. But is it fair to lay the blame on Albiera? If Piero—

ANTONIO: *(Losing patience.)* For the love of God! He already has a child!

BARTOLOMEO: *(Stunned.)* Piero?

ANTONIO: He had a child before he married. In the very year! *(Turns away.)* I don't condone him, of course. He devoted seven years to the study of law, and not one *day* to the study of discretion. On the other hand, I can't condemn him. I was young once myself. I know what happens when a spark flies too close to the kindling. And Piero was always—

(*Breaks off.*) Well, you know Piero. The trouble is that Albiera—out of despair for a child—grows stranger every day.

BARTOLOMEO: Stranger? What do you mean?

ANTONIO: (*Hesitates.*) I don't know what kind of priest you've become. Perhaps you won't agree. But in my opinion, Padre, she spends far too much time on her knees.

BARTOLOMEO: At prayer?

ANTONIO: She's not washing floors, I can promise you that. She prays, that's what she does, and meditates, and seldom eats. And when she is prevailed upon to eat, it only makes her ill. She needs a child, Padre, to draw her out of herself.

BARTOLOMEO: And she doesn't want Piero's child?

ANTONIO: She wants him desperately.

BARTOLOMEO: Then what's the problem? Children belong to their fathers—

ANTONIO: Piero won't hear of it. Not without the mother's consent, and we might as well howl at the moon. At one time I wouldn't have listened. I'd have done what I felt was right. But I can't go against him. Not on this issue. Not now. (*Turns to him.*) You have to persuade him, Padre. Or change the mother's mind. It's ripping us apart.

BARTOLOMEO: I see. (*Stands; moves away.*)

ANTONIO: I fear for Albiera, if she doesn't get that child. I fear for Piero, too. He doesn't know what's good for him, that boy. He never has. As for me, I don't mind telling you—(*Breaks off.*) I suppose I'm getting old. You can't imagine what it's like, to know I have a grandson living up that mountain— and the house an empty shell.

BARTOLOMEO: *(Pause.)* I'll speak to everyone involved. And weigh the facts. And pray to God for guidance. Then I'll tell you what I think is right—what I've come to believe is right. I make no promises, Antonio. I'll have to see.

ANTONIO: He's a remarkable child, Padre. I've never in all my life laid eyes on such a child. There's something about him that—defies description. We could give him opportunities. A future! Far more than he'll get up there. I don't believe we're being entirely selfish. I believe that Caterina is the one who's selfish. Wanting him all to herself. I believe if Piero would look at the child, if he could only be made to *look…*

BARTOLOMEO: *(After a moment.)* The mother's name is Caterina?

ANTONIO: Yes.

BARTOLOMEO: Not the Caterina who worked for you—five or six years ago?

ANTONIO: That's right, you'd remember her. Is something wrong?

BARTOLOMEO: *(After a struggle.)* When do you expect Piero?

ANTONIO: We don't expect him. He arrives when he arrives. That's Piero for you.

BARTOLOMEO: And Caterina. You've talked to her yourself?

ANTONIO: I've tried. The last time I saw her, do you know what she did? Slammed the door in my face. I offered her a dowry. Quite a generous one. In exchange for the child, you see. It's common practice in these situations, but—*(Breaks off.)* Caterina took it wrong. She has more pride than sense, that girl. I told her that. When Fortune comes to you, I said, and stares you in the eye, you grab her by the forelock—for by God she is bald at the back.

BARTOLOMEO: Where do I find Caterina?

ANTONIO: *(Stands.)* She works for Tommaso the Chatterer.

BARTOLOMEO: *(Surprised.)* He must have come up in the world.

ANTONIO begins to move off.

Antonio?

ANTONIO: Is there anything else, Padre? I don't mean to rush you, but I have a wall to build.

BARTOLOMEO: You don't mean to tell me that she's living in that— hovel!

ANTONIO: *(Uncomfortably.)* She's where she chose to be.

ANTONIO exits. BARTOLOMEO sinks into a chair and loses himself in thought. ALBIERA enters quietly and begins to collect the cups.

ALBIERA: *Scusatemi,* Padre.

BARTOLOMEO struggles to pull himself out of his thoughts.

You haven't finished your drink.

BARTOLOMEO: No.

ALBIERA: Would you like to?

BARTOLOMEO: No.

ALBIERA: I don't blame you. It's awful, isn't it? Francesco says it tastes like rabbit's pee.

BARTOLOMEO: I wonder how he knows.

ALBIERA: You will help us, won't you?

BARTOLOMEO: I suppose I have no option but to try.

ALBIERA: I know what you're thinking, Padre. You're thinking I'm spoiled. A spoiled and self-indulgent rich girl, who wants what she can't have. It isn't like that at all! I'd be a good mother to him. I'd love him as I would my own! There's so much we could give him. I don't mean only opportunities, I mean a family.

BARTOLOMEO: *(Studies her face.)* How old are you, Albiera?

ALBIERA: I've just turned twenty.

BARTOLOMEO: Twenty! But there's lots of time for children. Who's to say you won't have children of your own?

ALBIERA: I don't believe I'm meant to have them.

BARTOLOMEO: Why do you say that?

ALBIERA: In four years, Padre, I have never ceased to pray. I've prayed until my knees were raw. I've prayed until the floor in front of me was wet with tears. To no avail! I've been to doctors in Florence and Prato. All of them swore they could cure me, but after months of trying they threw up their hands. Then my sister Alessandra wrote to tell me of a remedy—a poultice that you lay across your belly. The woman who makes them swore she'd never put one on a wife who did not afterwards conceive—though she said they stink so much a lot of husbands throw them out before they can take effect. She promised to make one for me—this woman Alessandra knows—*(Beat.)* —but then she disappeared. Then a woman here in Vinci said to write my wishes on the inside of a belt, and ask a boy who was still a virgin to wear it on his naked flesh, after saying three Our Fathers and Hail Marys in honor of God and the Holy Trinity and St. Catherine—

BARTOLOMEO: *(Stands.)* Albiera—

ALBIERA: So I asked Francesco but he wasn't very keen. He said in any case he wasn't altogether certain that he was a virgin, so it likely wouldn't help. And then Antonio said it would be better to forget all that and simply feed three beggars on three Fridays, and not listen anymore to women's chatter. But either I find three beggars and it isn't Friday, or it's Friday and I can't find any beggars—

BARTOLOMEO: *(Touches her sleeve.)* I'm beginning to see what you mean. But, Albiera, you can't possibly conceive unless—*(Breaks off.)* Forgive me, but I understand Piero is mostly away.

ALBIERA: *(Glances at him; turns away.)* Who could blame him, Padre? A man needs a family. He tries to carry on as though it didn't matter, but it lies between us. Sorrow lies between us in the bed.

BARTOLOMEO: I see.

ALBIERA: I've been so desperate, Padre. You can't imagine the despair I've known. Sometimes I've wondered why I ever came into the world, and if—*(Beat.)* — and if it wouldn't do quite well without me. Then I realized the answer lay just up the mountain. The answer to everything!

BARTOLOMEO: For your sake, Albiera, let us pray that's true.

ALBIERA immediately drops to her knees and begins to pray.

I didn't actually—mean…

ALBIERA continues to pray. In prayer, she is beautiful and intense, as though lit by an inner flame. Perhaps she kneels in a beam of light. BARTOLOMEO watches her, entranced. At last she crosses herself, and stands.

ALBIERA: Thank you, Padre. I know that everything will work out now. You've set my heart at ease. *(Turns to leave.)*

BARTOLOMEO: But Albiera—I make no promises, you know.

ALBIERA: I feel your intention. That's enough.

BARTOLOMEO: And let's not forget Piero. You'd have to have his consent.

ALBIERA: *(With a childlike simplicity.)* How can he refuse—if Caterina tells you she will give me Leonardo?

ALBIERA exits, with the cups.

BARTOLOMEO: Leonardo.

CATERINA: *(Off.)* Leonardo!

BARTOLOMEO exits, on the run.

Scene VIII

A pine-shaded clearing beside a stream, up the mountain from Vinci. The same day, mid-afternoon. We hear the sound of water, tumbling over stones. If air could have a color, here it would be green. CATERINA, with her skirt tied up above her knees, sits watching Leonardo, off. Beside her lies a basket and a strange child-made contraption.

CATERINA: There it is! Jammed up against the bank. Just below those branches. See it? Over there! Straighten the sail a little before you set it afloat. That's it. That's right, that's better. Oh! Now watch it go! It sails like a dream, Leonardo. It sails as though it had wings!

BARTOLOMEO enters, mopping his brow.

It makes me think of a lark, you know? You should call it that. You should call your ship—*(Breaks off.)* Oh no. Well, it doesn't matter. It needs a rest, that's all. Set it on the shore and leave it for a while. Play with your kite instead.

BARTOLOMEO:	Caterina? I didn't mean to startle you. Do you remember me?
CATERINA:	Of course—Bartolomeo! A little the worse for wear.
BARTOLOMEO:	It's not a great distance, is it? But it's a steady climb. I'd forgotten what a climb it was. I've been away too long.
CATERINA:	You shouldn't have come in the heat of the day.
BARTOLOMEO:	Believe me, I know that now.
CATERINA:	Come and sit in the shade. *(Takes a cup from the basket; stands.)* I'll get some water for you.
BARTOLOMEO:	Don't bother, I can do it—

A waterfall appears. She fills the cup and gives it to him.

Thank you, that's very kind.

He sits and drains the cup. She remembers her skirt, unties it. Turns to check on Leonardo. Smiles. Waves at him.

You're looking well, Caterina.

CATERINA:	Am I?
BARTOLOMEO:	Very well. Motherhood agrees with you—
CATERINA:	*(To Leonardo, off.)* Let it out gently, Leonardo. Keep the ribbon taut. That's it. That's it. That's right. *(Follows the rise of the kite.)* Well done, Leonardo! Oh, just look at it soar! *(Glances at BARTOLOMEO.)* Look, Bartolomeo. He made it himself, you know.
BARTOLOMEO:	Did he? It's very well done. *(To Leonardo, off.)* Well done there, Leonardo!
CATERINA:	Say hello to Padre, Leonardo. *(Two beats.)* Sorry. He's playing shy.

BARTOLOMEO: He's a beautiful child, Caterina.

CATERINA: Thank you. He would be, though. They always are, it seems to me—the ones who are forged in heat.

BARTOLOMEO: *(Picks up the strange contraption.)* What's this supposed to be?

CATERINA: Listen to you change the subject.

BARTOLOMEO: Seriously.

CATERINA: I haven't figured it out yet. He's always making things. The game is to make me guess, you see, and gloat when I get it wrong. It's mostly toys he makes, but that one's something special. He calls it his first invention.

BARTOLOMEO: Where does he learn such words?

CATERINA: *(Hesitates.)* Oh, I suppose he had a little— prompting.

BARTOLOMEO: I see.

                They exchange a smile. She turns away to check on Leonardo.

CATERINA: It's odd that you'd appear like this—suddenly, out of the blue. I was thinking of you the other day. I was up to my elbows in laundry, and—*(Beat.)* — you suddenly came to mind.

BARTOLOMEO: That's not so strange. Laundry reminds me of you, as well.

CATERINA: It doesn't.

BARTOLOMEO: It does. A row of laundry, cracking in the wind? Caterina, every time.

CATERINA: *(Smiles.)* That was a lovely afternoon.

BARTOLOMEO: It was. *(Studies the contraption.)* I hadn't been ordained—

CATERINA:	Not quite.
BARTOLOMEO:	Not quite. And—oh, I don't know. I guess for me it was a kind of last flirtation. Before the door clanged shut.
CATERINA:	Well, if it had to be your last one, it's a good thing it was with me. I was such an innocent.
BARTOLOMEO:	You were.
CATERINA:	I fixed that soon enough, however.
BARTOLOMEO:	You did.

Both smile. A pause.

CATERINA:	Thank you, Bartolomeo.
BARTOLOMEO:	For what?
CATERINA:	For not chastising me. *(To Leonardo, off.)* Don't go too far, Leonardo. Bring it back this way.
BARTOLOMEO:	Why would I chastise you? I know who's at fault.
CATERINA:	*(Still to Leonardo.)* I want to be able to see you! That's the boy. *(Turns back to BARTOLOMEO.)* I'm sorry, what did you say?
BARTOLOMEO:	I said I know what this is. It's a kind of flying machine. A body would fit in here, you see? A body the size of a cat's. The feet here, the arms there. All made of wood and string. It's a little on the rough side, but you can see what he's getting at.

CATERINA takes the contraption, examines it, turns to Leonardo.

CATERINA:	Leonardo, your invention! Is it a flying machine? *(Two beats.)* Just look at him! He's grinning from ear to ear. *(Turns back.)* Well done, Bartolomeo. You're almost as clever as him. *(Studies the wings.)* It's remarkable, isn't it? I watch the swallows every

morning from my window. I watch them reel and dive. It lifts my soul to watch them. I long to soar like that. But I could never—never!—move from that longing to *this*. *(Pause.)* He's so bright, Bartolomeo. It's almost frightening. This afternoon, when we first got here, he found a shell that had turned to stone—lying by the stream. Where does it come from, Mamma? I didn't know what to say. I've found them often, here on Monte Albano. It hadn't occurred to me to wonder: how could they wash up so high? *(Beat.)* He sees things I don't even notice. He's forever asking *why*. Why, and how, and when, and where. How come, how come, how come! Sometimes I have the answer. Usually I don't. I just tell him he must learn to study nature. The answers must all be there.

> *She turns to find BARTOLOMEO watching her. She sets the contraption down.*

I'm sorry, Bartolomeo. I've been rude. I haven't asked you how you are. Or how long you'll stay.

BARTOLOMEO: I think I could stay here forever.

CATERINA: In Vinci, I mean.

BARTOLOMEO: Oh, not long, I suppose. They move us around so much. Just about the time you've come to know a parish, off you go again. Vinci is different, of course. Vinci will always be home.

CATERINA: *(Two beats.)* What's wrong with me? I wasn't thinking. I assumed you'd come for a visit.

BARTOLOMEO: I wish that were the case. I have to say it isn't easy, coming back here as the priest. Not that it's easy anywhere, but the stakes seem higher here. Where everyone knows me, you see.

CATERINA: *(Sits next to him.)* You'll be a great improvement.

BARTOLOMEO: Do you think so?

CATERINA: Definitely.

BARTOLOMEO: Then why do you look so glum?

CATERINA: *(To Leonardo, off.)* Away from the trees, Leonardo. You'll get all tangled up.

BARTOLOMEO: *(Still watching her face.)* Caterina?

CATERINA: *(Hesitates.)* You may be asked to get involved—in something that concerns me. I'd rather you didn't.

BARTOLOMEO: Too late.

CATERINA: *(Turns to face him.)* They've got to you already? It didn't take them long. What are you going to do about it?

BARTOLOMEO: What do you think I should do?

CATERINA: Tell them to go to hell.

BARTOLOMEO: Caterina.

CATERINA: Well, you asked.

BARTOLOMEO: *(Carefully.)* It's a complicated situation—

CATERINA: No, it's not.

BARTOLOMEO: *(Another try.)* You love your son, I can see that. Even so. There must be times when he's a burden to you—

CATERINA: Yes! A burden of joy.

BARTOLOMEO: You've said yourself he's clever. They could give him an education—

CATERINA: Oh! Is that what they say?

BARTOLOMEO: Yes, they do, they say—

CATERINA: They say a lot of things, those people. Yak yak yak.

BARTOLOMEO: I'm only trying to state their case.

CATERINA:	Leonardo is a bastard. You know what that means. He'll never go to university. They won't let him in. A career of any consequence will always be closed to him.
BARTOLOMEO:	There are other possibilities—
CATERINA:	Do you think I'd stand in his way? I wouldn't prevent them from helping. They can help him all they like. They don't have to take him from me!
BARTOLOMEO:	I didn't mean to upset you.
CATERINA:	I don't believe it's right. They have so much, and I have only Leonardo. My golden, golden son! He was a gift to me, a very special gift. I knew it when I carried him, long before the midwife laid him in my arms. I named him Leonardo, to give him strength, the strength of lions. He's going to need it. *(Struggles to stay in control.)* I bore him, and I named him, and I've cared for him. And now Antonio comes along and says he wants him. He thinks I should just—hand him over, like a calf. Well, I won't do it. I won't do it! How can they think I would? *(Struggles.)* They'd turn him against me, you know.
BARTOLOMEO:	I really don't think—
CATERINA:	They would! You can't trust them, Bartolomeo. Forgive me for saying it. *(Turns away.)* Besides, they don't deserve him. None of them deserve him. Not this child.
BARTOLOMEO:	*(Gently.)* I understand how you feel. But it's not for you to say what they deserve or don't deserve—
CATERINA:	*(Stands abruptly.)* Leonardo! Reel it in now, there's a good boy. It's time we were getting back.
BARTOLOMEO:	*(Stands.)* I don't know myself what's right. All I'm saying is this. Perhaps you should reconsider. For the sake of the boy, that is.

She turns on him.

I wish you wouldn't look at me like that.

CATERINA: Are you going to preach against me—like the last one did?

BARTOLOMEO: The last—?

CATERINA: Priest who came to Vinci. He held me up before the congregation—at the feast of Corpus Christi, when every seat was full. He held me up as an example.

BARTOLOMEO: Of?

CATERINA: Sin. Don't you see it on me? Burned across my forehead like a brand?

BARTOLOMEO: Of course not.

CATERINA: I'm surprised. He said that anyone who truly loved the Lord could see it there. He asked the members of the congregation who found they couldn't see it to leave the church at once. And no one did. So it seems odd to me that you can't see it. A man of the cloth, no less.

BARTOLOMEO: *(Uncomfortably.)* The Church's position on fornication—

CATERINA: It wasn't because I fornicated, it was because of my child. Because I refused to give him up. Antonio asked him to do it.

BARTOLOMEO: I can't believe that.

CATERINA: He did! And it's your turn now. Now you'll be doing his dirty work.

BARTOLOMEO: You shouldn't assume that.

CATERINA: *(Stares at him.)* I—what?

He knows he's offended her. He takes a step towards her.

Oh, no!

He freezes.

You've stomped right through his drawing. It was lovely, there in the dust.

BARTOLOMEO: I'm sorry. *(Turns to Leonardo.)* I'm sorry, Leonardo.

CATERINA: *(To Leonardo.)* Don't cry. You can make another one as soon as we get home. It will be—even better than this. Gather up your toys now. We have to go. *(Gathers their things.)*

BARTOLOMEO: Caterina, don't leave like this.

CATERINA: My father always told me to be wary of three things: the dithering of doctors, the platitudes of priests—and any man who says *you shouldn't assume that.* Do you know what that really means? It means you'll circle for a while and then you'll settle—like a fly!—where it's juiciest. I'm shocked, Bartolomeo. I thought you were better than that.

BARTOLOMEO: Caterina—

She exits.

Caterina!

BARTOLOMEO stares after her.

End of Act One.

Act Two

Scene I

The church in Vinci, the following Sunday. Spatters of sunlight here and there. A sense of soaring arches.

BARTOLOMEO: *(As an old man.)* Something happened to me that day. On the mountain, with Caterina. Something that's hard to explain. I'm not even sure how it happened. I know I was transformed. I returned to Vinci resolved—resolved!—to live as I ought to live. To be an inspiration—yes, I even thought that—to all my parishioners. I set to work on a sermon—my first one in Vinci as priest! I was determined to give them something they'd remember. It would have been better to give them something they'd forget.

We hear the sound of bells.

I won't inflict it all on you. Only the choicest parts.

BARTOLOMEO becomes young as he moves to the pulpit. He addresses the audience as though it were his congregation. He is visibly uncomfortable, refers frequently to his notes, etc.

The Bible says we should love God and keep ourselves in His grace. So I counsel you straightaway, as we gather together for the first time, to take your minds from earthly thoughts, no matter how pressing. For when men and women are in church to hear the divine service, their hearts should not be at home or in their fields, their minds should not be with any person or thing, but only with God. *(An attempt at humor.)* Remember the example of the man to whom a horse was promised if he could say a prayer and keep his thoughts on that alone, but who while praying wondered if the giver of the horse would give the saddle also—and so, unhappily, lost both. *(Smiles; waits expectantly; clears his throat.)* So it is with those who come to mass. After the mass, as you prepare to make your next confession, know this: that confession without contrition is unavailing. Contrition means sorrow of heart, it means coming before God in sincere repentance, concentrated wholly on your sins. These I urge you to lay out in a straight-forward manner, not putting the first last or the last first, neither excusing yourself nor accusing others. Simply tell the circumstances of your sins: where and when they occurred, how you have spoken of them since or committed them again—in other words, anything concerning them that burdens your soul. Finally, should you have any doubts as to how you have erred, I will now remind you of the seven deadly sins, from which all sins derive. But let me assure you that for each of these sins there is a virtue, which is contrary to the sin and fit medicine against it: for the sin of pride, humility; for the sin of envy, affection; for the sin of wrath, gentleness; for sloth, diligence; for avarice, generosity; for gluttony, temperance; for lechery, chastity.

> *He collapses into the confessional. ALBIERA enters and sits next to him.*

ALBIERA: Forgive me, Padre, for I have sinned. I'm guilty of the sin of envy. Just now I saw the cobbler's wife, lumbering down the aisle. The last thing she needs is another mouth to feed, but there she is, her belly all swollen—like an old wineskin full of new wine.

Wouldn't you think she'd be too old? She's thirty if she's a day.

BARTOLOMEO: My child—

ALBIERA: I know it was wrong, Padre—I know it was terribly wrong—but I couldn't help it. My heart welled up with envy. Why should she have babies every year and I be barren? Barren! It's such an ugly word.

BARTOLOMEO: *(Beat.)* Did you listen at all to the sermon?

ALBIERA: *(Uncomfortably.)* I tried.

BARTOLOMEO: If you'd tried a little harder you would know. There is a remedy for the sin of envy. *(No response.)* Well?

ALBIERA: I'm afraid my mind wandered a little.

BARTOLOMEO: The remedy for envy is affection. This is the virtue you will have to cultivate if you're going to overcome your impulse towards envy. Is there anything else you wish to confess?

ALBIERA: I don't think so, no.

BARTOLOMEO: Then this is what you must do. Whenever you feel a rush of envy towards another woman, you must immediately approach her and perform an act of kindness to cancel out your sin. Can you do this?

ALBIERA: To the cobbler's wife?

BARTOLOMEO: In this instance.

ALBIERA: But she's left already. Everyone has left!

He lets a silence grow. She struggles with herself.

However, I see what you mean. I see it, and I promise you—*(After another struggle.)* —I promise you I'll try.

BARTOLOMEO:	Bless you. A good deed is a good prayer, remember that. Say an Our Father and three Hail Marys as penance for your sin. Go in peace.

> *ALBIERA exits. BARTOLOMEO stands and exits.*

Scene II

> *The da Vinci garden, half an hour later. The apple trees bow low with fruit. Beneath them lies PIERO, fast asleep. BARTOLOMEO enters. He picks up the hammer and strikes the gong. PIERO springs awake.*

PIERO:	*Madonna serpente!*

> *They face one another. Beat.*

BARTOLOMEO:	I don't care for that expression.
PIERO:	I think I learned it from you.
BARTOLOMEO:	Don't use it in my presence, please.
PIERO:	Don't bang that wretched gong.
BARTOLOMEO:	It serves you right. You shouldn't be sleeping at this time of day. It isn't even noon.
PIERO:	Give me a little credit. I stayed awake in church. Which is more than most people did.

> *A direct hit. BARTOLOMEO falters.*

BARTOLOMEO:	I don't know what came over me.
PIERO:	Ah, it's nothing, you know. Look at it this way. Next week you can be very brief. You can stand up there and say: last week I told you everything you need to know about mass and sin and confession. I omitted nothing and since then nothing has changed. Therefore, make the sign of the cross and go in peace.

BARTOLOMEO: Very funny.

PIERO: I thought it was. It came to me as I was drifting off.

BARTOLOMEO: It's good to see you, Piero. I'd like to pound your face to sausage—

PIERO: Yes, I'm sure you would.

BARTOLOMEO: *(Beat.)* But it *is* good to see you.

PIERO: Likewise, you know.

An awkward pause.

I take it you've adapted to your calling. Your robe no longer chafes?

BARTOLOMEO: The wool is a little softer now, with wear.

PIERO: I often thought of you, these last few years, huddled in the confessional with your male parishioners. Asking impertinent questions.

BARTOLOMEO: I needn't have worried. It's not the men who come to confession.

PIERO: I see.

BARTOLOMEO: *(Beat.)* Your father tells me that your practice has expanded. You're doing well.

PIERO: *Documenti, documenti.* That's my life. It has its compensations though. It keeps me away from here. *(Before BARTOLOMEO can respond.)* Is there anything I can offer you? Lunch, perhaps?

BARTOLOMEO: All I want is an explanation.

PIERO: *(Beat.)* You asked too much of me.

BARTOLOMEO: I've heard a lot of lame excuses—

PIERO: It happens to be true. I tried to keep my promise. I swear to God I tried. I tried to get away from here, away from Caterina. I couldn't do it. She was like a madness on me, from the start. I couldn't get enough of her. Couldn't get enough! I used to wonder, sometimes, if she'd cast a spell on me.

BARTOLOMEO: Piero, for the love of God—

PIERO: Or maybe it was fate. *Provvidenza,* Padre! You ought to know about that. *(Two beats.)* I'm not as strong as you, Bartolomeo. I never have been, you know. That's why you're a priest and I'm a—I'm a—*(Breaks off.)* Whatever I am.

BARTOLOMEO: *(Carefully.)* You were always careless. Careless of other people, careless of consequence. But I never knew you to break your word. I counted on that. You made a promise—

PIERO: I did. Which I readily broke. I owe you an apology for that. If I give it to you now, will you accept it?

BARTOLOMEO hesitates.

You can't, can you? You sit in the confessional and you pardon perfect strangers. You can't do the same for me.

BARTOLOMEO: I'll tell you what sticks in my craw. To use her and discard her—as though she were nothing at all.

PIERO: It wasn't exactly like that.

BARTOLOMEO: No? How was it, then?

PIERO: I gave her up because my father begged me to—

BARTOLOMEO: Pregnant with your child.

PIERO: Come on, Bartolomeo, you know how it works. I had no more choice than you did after flaming what's-his-name—Saint Francis—dropped out of the sky—

BARTOLOMEO: Let's stick to the subject at hand.

PIERO:	*(Turns away.)* What was I supposed to do? Give up everything? All my prospects, all my father's grand ambitions? *(Beat.)* I used to think about it. I imagined going to her, trying to explain. Telling her I loved her, couldn't live without her, saw her face in my dreams! And all of it would have been true. But I never did it. Never went to see her. Haven't spoken to her since. *(Glances at him.)* That's something, at least. I didn't prowl around her after I was married. I'm not proud of my behavior, but I'm not—ashamed of that.
BARTOLOMEO:	You should have told me, should have written—
PIERO:	I intended to. I took up the pen a hundred times, but always my hand would freeze.
BARTOLOMEO:	I was bound to find out, sooner or later.
PIERO:	The later the better, for me.
BARTOLOMEO:	*(Two beats.)* Well, now you have a problem that you have to deal with.
PIERO:	Have I? Only one?
BARTOLOMEO:	I was referring to Leonardo.
	Beat. PIERO faces him.
PIERO:	Don't tell me they've got you involved in all that foolishness.
BARTOLOMEO:	Your father spoke to me. And also Albiera—
PIERO:	*Madre di Dio!* Every time I turn my back, they hatch another scheme. Stay out of it, Bartolomeo.
BARTOLOMEO:	I'd be happy to. But I've already told your father—
PIERO:	I don't understand it at all! Some priests are quite content to hand out candles and holy oil. We never seem to get those priests in Vinci. Why is that?

BARTOLOMEO: *(Lets this pass.)* One of the things I said I'd do—is have a talk with you.

PIERO: They want you to persuade me. Tell them you tried, and you can't. And that will be the truth. I won't do that to Caterina. I've told them again and again. That's another thing I've done that I am not ashamed of: I've stood firm on this.

BARTOLOMEO: *(Beat.)* What about Albiera?

PIERO: What about her?

BARTOLOMEO: Piero, don't be obtuse.

PIERO: I'm not convinced that Albiera won't have children of her own. The doctors could find nothing wrong. What she needs to do is put this fanciful— obsession over Leonardo completely from her mind.

BARTOLOMEO: And you think that you can live with Albiera, and your father—

PIERO: Don't worry, I just clear out.

BARTOLOMEO: I'm not sure that's the kindest thing—

PIERO: Kindest? Listen to me. I did what I was asked to do, when I was asked to do it. Now I do as I please.

BARTOLOMEO: I don't believe a word of that. That sounds like a pose to me.

PIERO turns away.

I hope I'm right about that. I'd like to think you were happy—

PIERO: I am, I'm very happy—when I'm not in Vinci.

ANTONIO appears in the distance.

I have to go.

BARTOLOMEO: You've only just arrived.

PIERO: Fishing, Bartolomeo. I'm meeting Francesco at the stream below the village. Why don't you come along? *(No response.)* If the catch is good, we'll have a feast tonight, to celebrate your return. *(Still no response.)* You'll have to forgive me sometime. You might as well do it now.

BARTOLOMEO: *(After a moment.)* How are they biting?

PIERO: They're not. They leap from the stream and arc through the air and land right smack in your lap. You just have to sit there and watch.

BARTOLOMEO: *(Unable to hold back a smile.)* I have some things I have to do. I'll join you later perhaps.

PIERO: Good man. *(Starts off; hesitates; turns back.)* I've always meant to ask you—your Saint Francis, when he dropped out of the sky. And told you you were needed. Did he happen to say what *for*?

BARTOLOMEO: I'm hoping that will be revealed to me.

PIERO: Hoping! You poor soul. You're just as trapped as I am.

BARTOLOMEO: I'm not trapped at all. I'm doing what I want to do. I haven't quite figured out why.

PIERO: *(Beat.)* I am glad you're back. I've missed you, my friend.

PIERO *exits.* ANTONIO *enters.*

ANTONIO: Bartolomeo—Padre! I didn't know you were here. *(Beat.)* That sermon this morning—

BARTOLOMEO: I know.

ANTONIO: Have you made any progress—?

BARTOLOMEO: Not yet.

ANTONIO: In that case, I'll just rush through. I have to harry the workmen. I'm still at work on that wall. *(Moves past him.)*

BARTOLOMEO: Antonio, this is the Lord's Day. Do you mean to tell me—

ANTONIO: Ah, look at it this way. The life of every man is short, and mine is almost finished.

BARTOLOMEO: But—

ANTONIO: Help yourself to the apples. They've just come ripe.

             ANTONIO exits.

BARTOLOMEO: Help yourself to the apples!

             BARTOLOMEO glances at the apples. Starts off. Reconsiders. Helps himself.

Scene III

The entrance to a house up the mountain from Vinci, twenty minutes later. A glimpse of towers and rooftops, poking through the August haze. A door, half open. CATERINA sweeps the step. ALBIERA enters, with flowers. She is flushed from exertion and giddy with excitement.

ALBIERA: Caterina? You don't know me, but my name is Albiera and I'm—

CATERINA: I know who you are.

ALBIERA: I'm so glad I found you. I didn't know where you lived, exactly, and I couldn't ask directions— someone would have stopped me—and I wasn't altogether certain—even though I've lived in Vinci for the last four years, I have to say I wasn't certain—*(A breath.)*—which mountain was Albano! I don't get out a lot, you see. I don't get out at all. Not on my own. Except for church. I used to see you there and once, when I was with Piero in the carriage, we passed you on the road. You were carrying your child, your Leonardo, and you looked—so beautiful, the two of you.

CATERINA: What are you doing here?

ALBIERA: *(Remembers the flowers.)* I came to give you these. I want you to have them, as a gift from Albiera. They looked quite lovely when I started out, but I can see I've lost some coming up the mountain. I was afraid they'd see me leave the village so I ran, you see, and I—I must have—well. They aren't as lovely as they were, but still—*(Presents them.)* — they're yours. Flowers, Caterina. From Antonio's garden! Take them, please.

CATERINA: No.

ALBIERA: Please. You have to take them.

CATERINA: No, I don't.

ALBIERA: You do! You must. I've come running up the mountain in the heat. To give them to you.

CATERINA: You didn't have to do that.

ALBIERA: Yes, I did. Padre Bartolomeo said I must!

CATERINA: So he's behind this.

ALBIERA: No! Well, yes. It's complicated. *(Catches a movement through the door.)* Is that your boy? *(Pushes forward.)* It's Leonardo, isn't it?

CATERINA: *(Barring her way.)* Get back!

ALBIERA: I only want a glimpse of him.

CATERINA: Take your flowers, do you hear me? Take your flowers and leave!

ALBIERA: *(Steps back; hesitates.)* I don't understand. We could be friends—

CATERINA: We can't be friends.

ALBIERA: We could if you were willing. I'd be willing. I wouldn't care what they said. I have no one, Caterina, not a soul. I hardly ever see my sisters anymore. I miss them, and I miss my mother. How I miss my mother! She—she always said I brought the sunlight with me when I walked into a room. But now I realize that's only how she saw me, it's not—how I really—*(Breaks off; swoons.)*

CATERINA: What's the matter? *(Steadies her.)* Albiera? I think you'd better sit down.

                > *A stool appears. CATERINA helps ALBIERA to sit.*

                Are you going to be all right?

ALBIERA: Oh yes, I'll just—if you don't mind I'll just relax a moment. Catch my breath. I let myself get too excited. Truthfully, I was scared. I couldn't think what I'd say to you, when I finally—could.

                > *CATERINA moves to the door. She addresses Leonardo, off.*

CATERINA: There are sticks in the basket. And a scarf on the chair. Invent a game, Leonardo. One you can play with your ball.

                > *She pulls the door nearly closed and turns to find ALBIERA staring off into the distance.*

ALBIERA: The view is nice from here. You can see the roofs of Vinci, from this spot. They're lovely, aren't they? In this light. Quite magical. *(Pause.)* What a fool I am. It didn't occur to me you'd hate me, but of course—why wouldn't you?

CATERINA: I really don't think you should be here.

ALBIERA: No, they wouldn't approve. They don't approve of anything I do. They don't even like me to pray! And sometimes I think they truly—truly!—would rather I couldn't speak. (Glances at her; smiles.) I don't mean to complain. They try to be kind, you know. But I don't think they've ever quite— resigned themselves to me. It was all a mistake, in a way. I was always going to join a convent. That was my childhood dream. But then Piero came to meet my sister Alessandra—and a miracle occurred. He walked right by her, just as though he didn't see her—the jewel of the Amadori sisters!—and he bowed, and kissed my hand. And I thought that God had spoken. And he looked so good to me! So I raised his chin and I—and I—happily agreed. It was months before I realized he chose me out of spite. To spite his father. Because he couldn't have you.

            CATERINA is dumbfounded. For her this is the dawning of a deep and unexpected pity. She takes a step towards ALBIERA.

CATERINA: Albiera—

ALBIERA: Don't say anything. Please! I don't want you to. I only want to sit here—just a little longer. Then I'll leave you in peace. (With a glance around.) It's lovely here. So quiet. Nothing in the air but birdsong. And my voice. (Pause.) It would have been better if he'd taken Alessandra. She was the proper choice. She's strong and beautiful and won't take any nonsense. She's a breeder too. I shouldn't use that word, I hate it. Why does it have to be? You're either a breeder, or you're barren. They both sound horrid to me.

            PIERO suddenly enters. ALBIERA leaps to her feet.

PIERO: (To ALBIERA.) I saw you running up the mountain.

I couldn't believe my eyes. What the hell do you think you're doing?

ALBIERA: I just—(*Raises the flowers.*)—I—

PIERO: You've gone too far, Albiera. This time you really have. I can't tolerate any more of this. It's finished, do you hear? You're not going to have Leonardo— now, or at any time. Once and for all, for the love of God, put it out of your mind! (*Beat.*) Now get on back to Vinci. And don't ever come here again. (*No response.*) What's the matter? Why do you stand there? What are you staring at?

> PIERO *moves to* ALBIERA, *seems about to grab her roughly, but restrains himself.*

I'll drag you down if I have to. Albiera? Move!

> ALBIERA *turns. The flowers fall at her feet. She sees them fall. She stumbles. He catches her.*

CATERINA: Be careful—

PIERO: Albiera, please don't do this. Here, I'll carry you.

> ALBIERA *pulls away from him. She walks unsteadily off. A pause.* PIERO *can't bring himself either to look at* CATERINA, *or to leave.*

Well, Caterina. Now you know. What a mess I've made of things. What a joke my life's become. You're well out of it, believe me. Ask anyone.

> He glances at her, then abruptly exits. CATERINA *stares after him. Then she kneels and begins, absentmindedly, to gather up the flowers. The door opens and a bright red ball rolls across to her.*

CATERINA: Oh look, a bright red ball! I can't imagine how it got here—(*Addresses Leonardo, off.*)—but it's exactly what I need.

> She picks up the ball and exits.

Scene IV

> *A bridge over a stream below Vinci, late that afternoon. FRANCESCO and BARTOLOMEO sit on the bridge, their bare feet dangling, holding fishing poles. The scene is lit by the reflection of the dance of sun on water, within a cathedral of trees.*

FRANCESCO: Ah, this is the life. Wouldn't you say so, Padre?

BARTOLOMEO: I would.

FRANCESCO: I used to envy Piero. Being the eldest, you know. I wouldn't trade with him now for all the wine in Tuscany. He has to do what's required of him. I get to do what I want.

BARTOLOMEO: How do you get away with that?

FRANCESCO: Nobody notices me.

BARTOLOMEO: I wouldn't go that far. I noticed, for instance, that you weren't in church this morning.

FRANCESCO: *(Glances at him; beat.)* This is where I worship, Padre. That doesn't offend you, I hope. I sit here and I watch the play of light on water. I smell the wind in the trees. Listen to the birds converse. There's nowhere like it on earth. You may not believe me when I say this, but I swear it's true. If you put your ear to the ground, just at the foot of the bridge, and concentrate your thoughts, you can hear the steps of everyone who's walked along here. Bianca taught me that.

BARTOLOMEO: You mean the one they called a witch?

FRANCESCO: Nobody understood. She was a midwife, and a healer. And something of a seer. If Bianca put her ear to the ground, just at the foot of the bridge, she could tell you not just everyone who'd walked along there, but who'd be passing next. You wouldn't think it possible. She could do it, though.

She could see the future on the face of anyone she met. People knew it too. They'd cover their heads when they saw her. We used to chuckle at that.

BARTOLOMEO: Where is she now, Bianca?

FRANCESCO: She came down with the fever, about a year ago. It took her fast. (Beat.) I miss her, you know. I learned a lot from her. I only wish I'd known her sooner. I wouldn't have known her at all, if it hadn't been for Caterina.

BARTOLOMEO: Caterina?

FRANCESCO: It was something she said. Just before we betrayed her. That's what we did, Padre. Make no mistake about that. Now they want to do it again. (Turns away in disgust.) I wash my hands of it! You can't take everything you want, just because you want it—and it's there. You have to show some restraint. That's what I believe. But nobody listens to me.

They fish for a moment in silence.

BARTOLOMEO: I wonder what's keeping Piero.

FRANCESCO: Someone waylaid him, no doubt. Someone wanting free advice. It happens all the time. He's tried to sneak into Vinci, but he's never been able to. Word gets around. It doesn't take forever, either. Bianca used to say in Vinci if you farted, half the population held its nose. (Glances at him.) She didn't mince words, Padre.

BARTOLOMEO: No.

FRANCESCO: I liked her for that.

Again, they fish in silence.

BARTOLOMEO: You're right about this place. It has a holy feel. It always did, I think. I used to come here often when I was growing up. It was here that—(Hesitates.)

—something happened. Something that changed my life.

FRANCESCO: If you mean your vision, Padre, I already know about that. I heard all about it over there, just at the foot of the bridge.

> *BARTOLOMEO turns to him in amazement. FRANCESCO laughs.*

Naw, Piero told me. I wheedled it out of him. You know what I thought when he told me? You poor son of a bitch.

> *Suddenly, off in the distance, church bells begin to peal.*

BARTOLOMEO: What on earth is that?

FRANCESCO: Something's happened in the village. It isn't good.

> *They stand, scramble to collect their things and exit on the run.*

Scene V

> *The da Vinci garden, half an hour later. The shadows are like velvet. A full moon rises in the distance, but as the scene progresses it is lost in cloud. ANTONIO paces. BARTOLOMEO and FRANCESCO enter.*

ANTONIO: It's Albiera. She tried to poison herself.

BARTOLOMEO: My—God!

ANTONIO: I found her lying over there. She's in a terrible way.

BARTOLOMEO: *(Starts off.)* I'll go straight up.

ANTONIO: You can't. There's been a complication of some kind.

BARTOLOMEO: *(Turns back.)* A what?

ANTONIO: They'll send for you, they said. *(Turns away.)* As long as I live, I'll never forget. Finding her lying there. That poor little—wraith of a thing…

BARTOLOMEO: What brought this on, does anyone know? And where is Piero?

ANTONIO: Piero is up there with her. He says it's all his fault.

BARTOLOMEO: His? How can it be?

ANTONIO: Exactly what I said. She was always fragile, always—deeply melancholic.

FRANCESCO: Father, that isn't true.

ANTONIO: *(As though he hasn't heard.)* The first time I looked at her, I thought: that girl is closer to the coffin than the cradle. I favored her sister, Alessandra—she's good meat with lots of flavor—but Piero wouldn't have her.

FRANCESCO: You're not going to start this again.

ANTONIO: I'd written him all about her! Get the jewels ready, I said, and let them be beautiful, for I have found you a wife! And he went to Florence and he walked right by the one I'd chosen for him, and he took Albiera's hand. What was he thinking about? You don't choose a wife the way you choose—an apple or a piece of cheese. Choose your wife and you choose your future! Everyone knows that.

            FRANCESCO stands abruptly. He addresses BARTOLOMEO.

FRANCESCO: Can I get you something, Padre? A little mulled marjoram?

ANTONIO: *(To BARTOLOMEO.)* Now he's mocking my marjoram.

FRANCESCO: A little rabbit's pee?

ANTONIO: *(Stands.)* I won't put up with this. Not in my house, not from my own children—

FRANCESCO: *(To ANTONIO.)* It's time to play the cards we've been dealt.

ANTONIO: *(To BARTOLOMEO.)* What is he talking about?

FRANCESCO: *(To BARTOLOMEO.)* I saw a peasant once get bitten by a viper. It got him on two fingers of one hand. He didn't hesitate. He took up his axe, put his hand on a stump and whacked the fingers off. He knew if he didn't he'd die. You see what I'm saying, Padre. He played the cards he was dealt. We need to learn to do that. All of us! It's when we don't that people get hurt. Women—especially!— get hurt. *(Gets himself in hand.)* I'm going to get some wine. Would you like some, Padre?

BARTOLOMEO: I don't think so.

FRANCESCO: *(To ANTONIO.)* Father?

                ANTONIO waves him away. FRANCESCO exits. Pause.

BARTOLOMEO: *(In an effort to distract him.)* Your garden is lovely in this light.

ANTONIO: Do you think so?

BARTOLOMEO: Yes. The shadows are like velvet.

ANTONIO: I'll tell you honestly, Bartolomeo, I don't know why I bother. I'm only building myself a hole—a fit little hole from which I'll soon be banished. I labor in this garden just as though it were the dwelling place of my immortal soul. And I know full well it's not! *(Glances at him.)* That's the sort of thing you should be pointing out to me. That's what priests are for!

BARTOLOMEO: *(Gently.)* We mustn't give up hope, you know.

PIERO enters, stops abruptly, and stands staring at them, dazed. FRANCESCO follows him on.

ANTONIO: Piero? Piero, what's wrong?

BARTOLOMEO: What is it? Is it Albiera?

PIERO: *(With a bewildered air.)* That girl—can you believe it? That girl—that girl!—was pregnant.

               Dead silence.

               She's lost it now, of course. She's gone and lost— *(His voice catches.)* —what she didn't know she had!

BARTOLOMEO: *(When this sinks in.)* How is she? How is Albiera?

PIERO: It's too soon to say. *(Turns helplessly to his father.)* She'll never have another chance, they say. Impossible.

ANTONIO: They can't be sure of that.

PIERO: Well, that's—what they say.

               ANTONIO wheels away.

FRANCESCO: Father, where are you going?

ANTONIO: I'm going to knock down a wall.

               ANTONIO exits. PIERO sinks into a seat.

PIERO: What a day it's been! One of those days when all your sins like pigeons come home to roost. *(With difficulty.)* I stood there today, up on Monte Albano—Albiera on one side of me, Caterina on the other. Do you know what I realized? I didn't deserve either one of them. What a surprise! It's always been the other way—somehow, in my mind. Who did I think I was? Whoever told me I was—I was—such a prize?

BARTOLOMEO: *(Takes a step towards him.)* Piero—

PIERO:	I've always been careless—you said it. Now what am I going to do? Give me an answer, someone. What do I do if she dies?
FRANCESCO:	She isn't going to die.
PIERO:	You sound so certain.
FRANCESCO:	She isn't because she wants to. And she never gets what she wants.
PIERO:	That's a joke, I take it.
FRANCESCO:	*(Turns away.)* I'm counting on that.
BARTOLOMEO:	We'll have to pray she lives, that's all. We'll just have to pray.
PIERO:	*(To BARTOLOMEO.)* Will you sit with me beside her? Pray for her there? I swear I can't sit there alone.

BARTOLOMEO lays an arm across PIERO's shoulders. They exit.

Scene VI

A room in the da Vinci house, the following evening. Candlelight.

| BARTOLOMEO: | *(As an old man.)* It's here that I often stumble— when I think about that time. I don't know what it is. There are things I remember so clearly. Things I completely forget. Everything is jumbled in my mind. |

A bed appears, with ALBIERA in it. A chair on either side. PIERO sits in one of them.

I know the night passed, and a day, and another night began—while Albiera hung suspended between life and death. I know I sat beside her bed and prayed for her. And prayed and prayed and prayed. I was convinced that if I didn't pray, she'd die. She lay in a restless stupor, though at times she'd wake.

ALBIERA: When will they ring the bells?

BARTOLOMEO: —she'd cry.

ALBIERA: When will they ring the bells? Two for a woman, three for a man, but what for a suicide?

BARTOLOMEO: She'd drift into a kind of sleep, then wake and say instead—

ALBIERA: Don't let them ring the bells for me. I don't want the bells! May He who died on the rood tree grant me this.

BARTOLOMEO: And then she'd ask for Piero.

ALBIERA: Piero?

BARTOLOMEO: And Piero was always there.

In the distance, we hear the sound of wind.

The weather turned. The heat broke and a wind came up. A high and whining, irritating wind. It shook the house.

A high and whining, irritating wind pounds against the house. BARTOLOMEO becomes young. He takes a seat beside ALBIERA's bed and bends his head in prayer. ALBIERA stirs. BARTOLOMEO looks up to find her watching him.

ALBIERA: You keep praying for me, Padre. Am I going to die?

BARTOLOMEO: Not if God will listen to me.

ALBIERA: Sssh! Don't bother God.

BARTOLOMEO: Not if you make up your mind to live. That's what you have to do. Do you hear me, Albiera? Albiera!

PIERO: Bartolomeo—she's asleep.

BARTOLOMEO: *(Takes a closer look.)* Of course she is.

PIERO: Why don't you go home? Get some sleep yourself.

BARTOLOMEO: No, I have to pray.

PIERO: You've said enough prayers to save the whole of Christendom. Go home, and get some rest. I'll send for you if I need you. Please.

                BARTOLOMEO nods his head. He stands.

                You'd better hurry. It's starting to rain.

                BARTOLOMEO exits.

Scene VII

                The vestry at Vinci, immediately following. The clatter of wind-driven rain. BARTOLOMEO enters to find CATERINA there. She's beside herself.

BARTOLOMEO: What are you doing here? It's pouring rain.

CATERINA: I have to know if she's all right.

BARTOLOMEO: *(Hesitates.)* She's alive…

CATERINA: Then she's all right.

BARTOLOMEO: It's too soon to say.

CATERINA: She could die.

BARTOLOMEO: She could, you see, she—*(Hesitates.)*—could.

CATERINA: I need your help, Bartolomeo. I don't know what to do. I know I ought to pray she'll live. I ought to, but I can't! If she lives they're sure to take my Leonardo. Because of the baby she's lost. Even Piero—Piero—will bow to their arguments now.

So I ought to pray that she'll die, you see. But how could I live with myself? And yet it would save me—would save me—

BARTOLOMEO: What are you talking about?

CATERINA: Bartolomeo, don't you see? If Albiera dies, then Piero could remarry and have children, and Antonio would have his heir—his precious heir!—and not bother anymore with Leonardo. So I really need her to die! And yet I don't want her to. I feel such pity for her. I never thought I'd live to say that, but—*(Struggles.)*—I do.

BARTOLOMEO takes her hands.

BARTOLOMEO: There's only one prayer, Caterina. And that is that God's will be done.

CATERINA: I don't think I can pray for that. I have an awful feeling that this God of yours has already taken sides.

BARTOLOMEO doesn't answer. He studies her hands.

It would break my heart to lose my Leonardo.

BARTOLOMEO: I know it would.

CATERINA: I don't how I'd live without him. He's brought me so much joy!

BARTOLOMEO kisses her hands.

I couldn't bear to have him turned against me.

BARTOLOMEO: That wouldn't happen.

CATERINA: It would! I know it would because I've dreamt about it—over and over again! I've tried not to give it credence, but it plays on my mind. *(Gathers her strength.)* I've dreamt I'm an old, old woman—

standing in a room I've never seen. And over there, behind a door that leads—to what? I'll never know—is Leonardo. My son, my light, my golden Leonardo—now a full grown man. I know he's there because the door has just slammed shut. He's angry with me. He's so angry I can feel it through the door. I run to it, I try to open it, it's locked. He's locked the door behind him! Why, to keep me out? I pound on the door. Why are you angry with me, Leonardo? What have I done? At first there's silence only, then the door swings open and he's standing with the light behind him—glaring down at me. *(In a different voice.)* I don't want you following funerals. It's embarrassing, the mother of Leonardo traipsing through the streets behind a corpse. Stay home, don't make a spectacle, I'll give you money if you need it, is that what you do it for, the money? *(In her own voice.)* Then I say the thing that drives him mad. Let me go home, Leonardo. Let me go home, I beg you! I don't belong in this place. That's when it happens—an explosion. As though a window opens up inside his mind and all the fury he's been storing up in there comes pouring out. How I never loved him. How I abandoned him. Gave him up without a word into his father's keeping. Without a word! Can such a thing be true? I want to tell him: Leonardo, think about it! Can such a thing be true? But before I say a word he turns away, he slams the door, I hear the key turn in the lock, I hear the lock—click shut and I'm left standing, standing—standing in a room—I don't know where it is!—beside a door, a door I know is locked—to me! *(Struggles for control; turns to him.)* You've got to help me, Bartolomeo. If Albiera lives, you've got to warn me. Give me a little warning, so that I can—*(Breaks off.)*

BARTOLOMEO: So that you can what?

CATERINA: Run away!

BARTOLOMEO: *(After a struggle.)* I'll pray for guidance, Caterina. That's all I can promise you.

CATERINA: Thank you, Bartolomeo. *(Starts off.)*

BARTOLOMEO: Don't go yet, Caterina. Wait! At least until the rain lets up—

              But she is gone.

Scene VIII

              The church in Vinci, half an hour later. BARTOLOMEO kneels, deep in tortured prayer. Outside, the storm rages.

Scene IX

              The vestry, the following morning. The rain has stopped, but the wind still blows; we hear a shutter bang. BARTOLOMEO is at prayer. PIERO enters. He stands watching BARTOLOMEO, who finally looks up.

BARTOLOMEO: Piero! *(Stands.)* I didn't hear you knock.

PIERO: I didn't knock.

              A shutter bangs violently, off.

              There didn't seem much point.

BARTOLOMEO: How is she this morning?

PIERO: Much improved.

BARTOLOMEO: Is she? Thank God.

PIERO: I think it's you we have to thank.

BARTOLOMEO: No, no. No! Not me.

              The wind howls.

PIERO:	Listen to that, would you? Have you ever heard such a wind? They tell me there are trees down all the way to Montelupo. It's like a battleground. *(Glances around.)* We haven't exactly spoiled you, have we? Not even a decent chair.
BARTOLOMEO:	It doesn't matter in the least.
PIERO:	*(Beat.)* I think you know why I've come. I have to take Leonardo. There's no avoiding it now. You can see that I have to, can't you?
BARTOLOMEO:	To ease your conscience?
PIERO:	No! *(Beat.)* Yes, of course, to ease my conscience. But it isn't only that. To mend the marital cloth— while there's something left to mend. To put this business behind us. To finish it, once and for all! *(Beat.)* I want you to set the terms. Be a little extravagant. Set Caterina up as well as you are able. Secure her future, all right? My father doesn't need to know I said that. You know what I'm saying, I think.
BARTOLOMEO:	*(After a long moment.)* You're the notary, Piero. What would be reasonable?
PIERO:	The standard rate is twenty florins—
BARTOLOMEO:	Twenty!
PIERO:	More or less. More for a boy than a girl, of course. More for a healthy child.
	A sudden calm.
	Listen, did you hear that? The wind's gone down. It was there, and then it wasn't. Isn't that strange? *(Studies his hands.)* This is a difficult business.
BARTOLOMEO:	It is.
PIERO:	*(Stands.)* I'll throw my support behind you,

whatever terms you set. Please do it quickly. Today.

PIERO exits.

Scene X

A road up the mountain from Vinci, moments later. Aftermath of a great storm. BARTOLOMEO climbs the mountain. CATERINA suddenly enters.

CATERINA: I was standing at the window and I saw you coming. I think I know what this means.

BARTOLOMEO: I've been asked to set the terms. I said I would—to buy you time. There isn't a lot of it, though. I'll have to see them later today.

CATERINA: I'm already packed. I'll tell Leonardo we're going on a great adventure—*(Breaks off; beat.)* How can I thank you for this?

BARTOLOMEO: That's easy. Pray for me.

CATERINA: You don't need my prayers.

BARTOLOMEO: I need all the prayers I can get. Now, especially.

He begins to move off. She stares after him. He stops moving, turns back to her.

Caterina—*(Breaks off.)* You will take care of yourself?

CATERINA exits.

Scene XI

The da Vinci garden, late that afternoon. Everything is burnished by the sun. BARTOLOMEO enters. He strikes the gong. He sits. He stands. He paces. He strikes the gong again. Finally he beings to bang the gong, wildly and insistently. PIERO, ANTONIO and FRANCESCO enter.

ANTONIO: All right, all right, we hear you!

Now that he has their attention, BARTOLOMEO hesitates.

PIERO: Go ahead, Bartolomeo. State the terms.

BARTOLOMEO: There aren't going to be any terms. You're not going to have Leonardo. Not at any price.

PIERO: What are you talking about?

BARTOLOMEO: Caterina is gone. She took the boy, Leonardo, and she ran away. Quite early this morning. She'll be far from here now.

Two beats.

FRANCESCO: You knew she was going?

BARTOLOMEO: I did.

PIERO: You knew she was going, and you didn't stop her?

ANTONIO: Didn't tell us?

BARTOLOMEO: I tipped her off.

PIERO: No, you didn't.

BARTOLOMEO: I did, Piero. I did—and I'll tell you why. Because you don't deserve him. I don't believe you deserve him. Any of you. You're all just—*(With an extravagant gesture.)*—fumbling around! Tossing blame at one another, like an egg no one wants to drop. Thinking a child will solve your problems. But who's to say it will? What happens if it doesn't? Who do you blame *then*, the child? And meanwhile up there on that mountain is a woman—*was* a woman—*(Breaks off.)* Do you know what she is? Have you actually talked to her? Have you seen her with that child? There isn't one of you who's thinking clearly. It's as though you're all caught on a wheel. Caught on a wheel that just keeps turning, and you're powerless. You can't stop it, and you can't get off. You can't do anything. Well, I've stopped it, do you hear me? I've finally stopped the wheel.

Pause.

And even as I say this I know, in my heart of hearts—I'm not any better than you. Like you, I've been fumbling around. I've handled all of this badly. I've done the cowardly thing. *(To PIERO.)* I could have told you this morning you shouldn't have the child. Instead I went sneaking up the mountain. Like a traitor, behind your back. I'm sorry for that. Truly sorry. It was wrong of me.

PIERO: Do you think you can just say that, and be done with it?

BARTOLOMEO: *(As though he has been struck.)* No! I don't think that at all. *(Sinks into a seat.)* I've been walking most of the day. I don't know how far I've walked. Trying to come to terms with what—with what—*(Breaks off.)* With what my life's become. *(With great difficulty.)* I never thought I'd be a great priest. Never imagined that! But I've hoped—I've prayed—dear God, how I've prayed!—simply for the grace to be a good one. Only that. Surely if you've had a vision, if you've—by some amazing chance—found yourself touched that way. Surely to be a good priest is not too much to ask. But I'm not even that.

FRANCESCO: Padre—

BARTOLOMEO: I don't know what to do except to ask for your forgiveness. And speak to the bishop, of course. Perhaps he'll send me to another parish. I don't know what he'll do.

FRANCESCO: Padre, if you ask me—

ANTONIO: No one's asking you.

FRANCESCO: I'm saying it anyway. *(To BARTOLOMEO.)* I don't care what the bishop says, I can tell you this. A priest who is less than perfect is a comfort to his congregation. That's a fact of life.

FRANCESCO moves away. Long pause.

PIERO: What the hell do I tell Albiera? *(Stands.)* That's what I'd like to know.

PIERO moves away. Another pause.

ANTONIO: All this heartache, when you think about it. All for a little boy. *(Moves next to BARTOLOMEO.)* Look at it this way. Things could always be worse. You could be the priest at San Martino. Haven't you heard? Homes destroyed, hay scattered, peasants working in the fields—completely swept away! The bell tower was reduced to rubble, and the bells—bells the size of barrels, Padre!—scattered throughout the fields. They're calling it a hurricane. A hurricane in Tuscany! You see what I'm trying to say. What's one boy—*(Begins to falter.)*—one little boy… compared to all of that?

              CATERINA enters. They gradually become aware of her presence, and turn towards her. She gathers her courage to speak. Towards the end of her speech, "The Last Supper" reappears on the upstage wall. For a brief moment, her position echoes that of Christ; the men's positions echo those of some of the disciples.

CATERINA: When Leonardo was a baby—barely five months old—I woke one day to find him looking at me. Lying in his cradle, looking at me—with my father's eyes. Everything was there. The love, the wit, the tenderness. And a kind of ancient sorrow, a deep, abiding—*human* sorrow, as though he saw the future, and it wasn't pretty, and was somehow—painfully familiar with the past. I picked him up. I hugged him. I danced him around the room. And when I looked at him again, all of that was gone. He was just my Leonardo, looking back at me. With his own familiar eyes. And I wondered if I'd imagined it. But how was that possible? Then who was this child who looked at me with a wisdom he shouldn't have? *(Pause.)* From the start, from the very beginning, I knew he was a gift. More than a gift—a treasure—that God had given me. A kind of compensation—this is what I told myself—for the things I couldn't have. But I had no right to think that. Who was I to say?— that others have more while I have less. That he was only mine. *(Struggles to stay in control.)* When my father was dying, he told me: Caterina, I know you're in pain. I've been trying to think what to say to you, and it finally came to me. The thing we feel we can't endure is the thing we must embrace. I've never forgotten that. It's such an elegant response, he said, I'm sure God would endorse it. It was his last gift to me. *(Two beats.)* You see, I'm speaking of gifts. Not pain or loss or—*(Breaks off.)* Gifts! *(After another struggle.)* He's a very inquisitive boy. He'll pester you with questions. You must always answer him as truthfully as you can. And then be prepared for more. If he makes something you've never seen, and asks you to guess what it is, study it carefully. Take time to give him an answer. It might be a flying machine. He has a—has a—bag of toys. And things he's made for himself. I'll bring them down to you. And a book he doesn't understand. It's time he learned to read. I hope you'll teach him that. I hope you'll teach him— everything! He'll keep you all on your toes. Leave a candle burning in his room at night. He's sometimes a little afraid. If he cries—if he cries— just hug him. And tease him when he pouts. And make sure he finishes what he starts. Then praise him to the skies.

She is unable to go on. After a moment, she exits. No one moves. Finally BARTOLOMEO turns to the others. He is utterly astounded.

BARTOLOMEO: Do you see—do you see—what she did?

ANTONIO: She gave us Leonardo, Padre!

BARTOLOMEO: More! Even more than that.

The da Vinci garden begins to fade away. "The Last Supper" glows as though lit from behind by a blazing, golden light.

Scene XII

The refectory of the monastery of Santa Maria delle Grazie in Milan. Early evening. BARTOLOMEO, as an old man, stands before the painting. We hear the sound of bells. He faces the audience.

BARTOLOMEO: *Sentite! Il vespero!* The call to vespers. All over the monastery, now, the monks have raised their heads. Turned their ears towards the sound. In a moment, if you listen closely, you'll hear the clapclapclap of bare feet on cold stone: the monks, moving down the stairs and hallways on their way to chapel. It's a sound I've grown to love, that whispering clapclapclap, since I became a fixture here. The Unmovable Irremovable One, the Prior likes to say. He doesn't really mind. The life of every man is short, and mine is almost finished. I seem to have heard this before. If I choose to spend what's left of it—(*Gestures towards the painting.*) —contemplating miracles, wouldn't it be churlish to complain?

He turns back to the painting. In the distance, very faintly, the monks begin to sing.

I come here and I stand before this painting. I see a
whole string of them! The painting itself. The artist.
He may have been illegitimate, but I can tell you:
he was no accident! The miracle of love. The
miracle of being young and open to possibility in
that golden time. And most of all—I hope you'll
forgive my bias—the miracle of Caterina. Who
blessed us with her sacrifice. And illumined all my
days… *(Trails off.)* Oh yes, there's quite an array. It
fills my heart to see it. Miracles abound.

> *He loses himself in contemplation of the painting.*
> *The singing swells and grows until we feel as*
> *though we're sitting in a grand cathedral.*

The End